CLASSIC

MARY BERRY

BBC BOOKS

Introduction

The recipes in this new collection lie at the very heart of my cooking. They are my essential dishes – those that will always be in my repertoire. With their winning combination of delicious ingredients, it's a pleasure to cook and serve them as I know they will always go down well, guaranteed to put a smile on the faces of family and friends.

FOR ME ingredients are the star of the show and a classic dish is one that shows them off to their best advantage, with the maximum flavour and minimum of fuss. Simplicity is the key, reflected in our own national cuisine – age-old dishes that have been handed down through the generations. Think of a simple roast bursting with glorious flavour, accompanied by a delicious array of fresh vegetables; stews and casseroles that become meltingly tender after long, slow cooking in the oven; or a seasonal fruit-based pudding like a tart or fool. The green and fertile farmlands of the British Isles are the perfect environment for producing high-quality vegetables and meat – a source of inspiration for many of the recipes in this book, such as the Cannon of Lamb with Minted Spring Vegetables on page 129 or the Roast Chicken Thighs with Sweet Potato & Cauliflower on page 73, not to mention the sustaining soups and other vegetable-based dishes included here.

My husband Paul and I grow much of what we eat and so I'm always using fresh produce from the garden – whatever is in season. If there is a glut of fruit, then a classic crumble immediately comes to mind. I've included a plum crumble here (page 213), as I love the combination of the tart fruit and crumbly topping, but any other fruit would do. Apples are perfect for a Tarte Tatin (page 205), that 'upside down' French classic, or a combination of apples and pears for a strudel (page 201) – a very popular pudding at one stage and now making a well-deserved comeback. When rhubarb is in season, I'll make a Ginger & Rhubarb Chilled Cheesecake (page 228) or, for something a bit different, the Rhubarb & White Chocolate Mousse on page 223, both ideal for entertaining as they can be made ahead and kept in the fridge until needed the next day.

Fruit goes beautifully with meat too, of course, giving a lovely sharp but sweet contrast in an otherwise savoury dish. It works particularly well with game, I find, such as in the Slow-Roast Duck with Pork & Cherry Sauce on page 91 – a classic combination but also a change from the more familiar Duck à l'Orange – the Roast Partridge with Plum Sauce (page 99) or the Pot-Roast Pheasant with Calvados (page 94), with apple slices fried in butter and added to the pot just before serving.

Today there seem to be so many different ingredients to choose from, new foods from every corner of the globe, that it's easy to forget that our national dishes have always been influenced by the cuisine of other countries. Many of our modern British classics, some of which have been around for decades, originate in other parts of the world. Lasagne, which I've included on page 140, is an Italian classic really, but now it's most definitely a British classic too! Kedgeree (page 46), a big favourite of mine, was originally an Indian dish, of course, but it's been a British classic since Victorian times. For me nothing beats that wonderful combination of taste and texture: the smoky fish and spiced rice with the soft-boiled egg and fried onion topping. As a nation, we love our curries, and I've included a chicken-based one here (page 79) – very popular with my family too, particularly with Paul, who lived in Malaysia for a time in his youth.

Over the years that I've been cooking, so many recipes have come and gone, and it's wonderful to see a few neglected classics making a comeback. Prawn Cocktail (page 38) is such a great combination of ingredients, and so easy to knock up for a starter. Toad in the Hole, perfect to feed the family, is both tasty and very economical. To breathe new life into the old classic, I've baked individual 'toads' and served them with onion gravy (page 112), which would otherwise go beautifully with the Jumbo Bangers with Cheesy Mash on page 110. There are one or two overlooked desserts here too, such as the Lemon Syllabub on page 247, for instance. Fresh and delicate, it uses only four ingredients and is so straightforward to prepare, perfect for rounding off a special meal. And for sheer decadence there's nothing quite like Banoffee Pie (page 233), invented back in the 1970s and now very much a classic of our time.

For chocoholics, there are meltingly delicious brownies (page 217), that almost no menu would be without these days, or the divine Chocolate Truffle Pots on page 240. I remember making these when I was first married! There are some lovely teatime treats here too. In addition to gloriously gooey flapjacks and melt-in-the-mouth shortbread (the quintessential biscuit, for me), there are some other revived classics: Chocolate & Vanilla Swirl Cake (or marble cake, page 283), Honey Melts (page 293) and Feathered Iced Biscuits (page 288) – all guaranteed to please.

While many of the dishes here are made with a timeless combination of ingredients that simply can't be improved upon, other recipes have been given a little twist. The Wild Mushroom Galettes on page 168 are my take on vol-au-vents, which used to be so popular as a starter or canapé. With their meaty-textured mushrooms, light flaky pastry and deliciously creamy sauce, they are impossible to resist! In a similar vein are the Little Passion Meringue Tartlets on page 210 – each like a mini Lemon Meringue Pie (page 198) with passion fruit added to the lemon curd for a variation on a very classic theme.

Other classics have been updated a little to suit modern life and tastes, and to make them fuss-free. See page 130 for beef burgers served in brioche buns with a healthy and delicious side

of carrot and beetroot slaw, or the Chicken, Avocado & Bacon Salad on page 82 – a truly classic combo and ideal for a light lunch. The Baked Fennel Gratin with Mascarpone (page 181), meanwhile, is a bit like dauphinoise potatoes but much quicker to prepare and with fewer carbs. Healthy and full of flavour and crunchy texture, stir-fries have become classics of our time – see the Pork Sichuan Noodles on page 114, for instance, or Vegetable Stir-Fry on page 167. And while nothing beats a good mash, it doesn't have to be confined to just potato – you can swap in swede or celeriac, for instance, or jazz it up with other tasty extras (page 177).

Included here are a few dishes that may be more familiar as something you would eat out, such as the Eggs Benedict with Spinach on page 33 or Sirloin Steaks with Béarnaise Sauce on page 133. They are both so delicious that they are well worth a try at home, and you'll learn how to make two classic sauces into the bargain: hollandaise as well as Béarnaise. For the English muffins for the Eggs Benedict, why not have a go at making your own? You'll find a recipe for them in the Teatime chapter of this book, along with a couple of other old-fashioned classics – Drop Scones and Rock Cakes (pages 261, 286 and 284).

While some of the recipes here may seem a little daunting at first glance, I've tried to give as much guidance as possible both in the method and in any tips. At the end of every recipe you'll find at least one tip, and I've also including cooking and chilling times to give you an idea of how long a dish is likely to take. Making one's life easier by preparing as much as one can in advance has been a long-time mantra of mine. You'll find that many elements of even the most time-consuming dishes can be made ahead and stored in the fridge or freezer. The Beetroot Gravadlax on page 41, for example, can be made and frozen well in advance, then defrosted for a delicious and colourful starter, while the Apricot & Brandy Ice Cream Bombe on page 229 is perfect for the busy Christmas period as it can be made up to a month ahead and simply brought out with a flourish to serve to family and friends.

In every chapter of the book, I've tried to include something for everyone and to suit every occasion, from canapés and light lunches to comforting family meals and impressive dishes to wow your guests. I've so enjoyed putting them together, becoming reacquainted with old favourites from the past and discovering ways of rejuvenating them for a new generation. I do hope you'll enjoy them too, and add them to your repertoire – maybe even start building up your own classic collection.

Mary Berry

CANAPÉS

·

FIRST COURSES

Olive Flatbreads with Hummus

SERVES 8 / PROVING TIME: 1½–2 hours / COOK TIME: 20–25 minutes

500g (1lb 2oz) strong white
  flour, plus extra for dusting
1 x 7g packet of fast-action
  dried yeast
4 tbsp olive oil, plus extra
  for greasing
350ml (12fl oz) warm water
75g (2½oz) pitted black
  olives, roughly chopped
Salt and freshly ground
  black pepper

For the topping
1 garlic clove, crushed
3–4 tbsp olive oil
6 sprigs of rosemary
Sea salt flakes

For the hummus
1 x 400g tin of chickpeas,
  drained and rinsed
1 garlic clove, crushed
Juice of ½ lemon
6 tbsp olive oil
3 tbsp natural yoghurt

This is a sociable starter and a real classic of our time, especially lovely with the olives running through and the rosemary topping. The vacuum-packed olives are soft and delicious, better than the pitted olives in brine in a jar. The addition of yoghurt to the hummus makes it particularly light and creamy, with a pleasant sharpness. Very more-ish!

1. To make the dough for the flatbreads, put the flour in a free-standing food mixer, or in a mixing bowl, and place the yeast on one side of the bowl and 1 teaspoon of salt on the other (see tip). Gradually add the oil and water and mix together until combined, either in the food mixer using the dough hook or by hand. Continue to knead on a low speed in the food mixer for about 10 minutes, or for 10–15 minutes by hand, until smooth, soft and glossy in texture, but still slightly sticky.

2. Grease a large bowl with oil. Add the dough, cover with cling film and leave to rise for 1–1½ hours or until doubled in size.

3. Tip the dough on to a floured work surface, knead for a minute or so to knock out the air and then divide into eight pieces. Roll out each piece thinly until it is about the size of your hand. Place some olives in the centre of each piece of dough, then fold the dough over the olives and seal the edges to make a ball. Turn each ball over so the seam is underneath and re-roll into a rough circle or oval shape.

4. Line two baking sheets with baking paper, dust with flour, then sit the dough pieces on top and leave to prove for about 30 minutes in a warm place.

Continued overleaf →

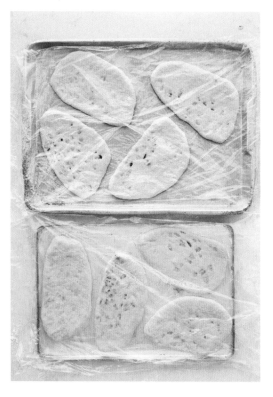

5. Preheat the oven to 220°C/200°C fan/Gas 7.

6. To make the topping, mix the garlic and oil together in a bowl, then brush over the flatbreads and poke small sprigs of rosemary at intervals into the dough. Scatter with sea salt flakes, bearing in mind that the olives are already salty.

7. Bake in the oven for 20–25 minutes until golden and slightly puffed up.

8. To make the hummus, place all the ingredients in a food processor, season with salt and pepper and whizz until fairly loose, smooth and creamy in texture. Spoon into a serving bowl (see tip).

9. Serve the flatbreads in slices ready to dip into the bowl of hummus.

Prepare Ahead:
The bread is best eaten fresh, although day-old bread will just be slightly firmer and drier for dipping on the following day. Just reheat until warm. The hummus will keep in the fridge for 1–2 days (see tip).

Mary's Classic Tips:
* Cover the hummus with a layer of olive oil or cling film in the fridge to prevent exposure to the air, which causes the hummus to darken.
* Sprinkle the finished hummus with paprika to give a little colour and extra flavour, if you like.
* Keep yeast and salt separate as salt kills yeast if they are in direct contact.

Grilled Asparagus with Garlic & Parsley Dip

SERVES 6–8 / COOK TIME: 5–8 minutes

1kg (2lb 3oz) large asparagus
    spears, woody ends
    snapped off (see tip)
Olive oil, for greasing and
    drizzling
50g (2oz) Parmesan cheese,
    grated
Salt and freshly ground
    black pepper

For the dip
4 tbsp full-fat mayonnaise
200ml (7fl oz) full-fat
    crème fraîche
1 fat garlic clove, crushed
1 tbsp chopped
    flat-leaf parsley

....

Prepare Ahead:
The asparagus can be boiled
ready for the grill up to 4
hours ahead. If preparing
ahead, make sure the
asparagus is refreshed in cold
water until stone cold to stop
cooking, then dry before
arranging on the platter.

Lucy's favourite of all the classic recipes. The British asparagus season is a real treat so over-indulge! A lovely, simple dish that makes the best of in-season asparagus.

1. Bring a shallow saucepan of salted water to the boil. Add the asparagus, bring back to boil and then boil for 2–3 minutes (depending on the thickness of the spears) until just tender – you want them to remain fairly firm (see tip). Drain and run under cold water for a few seconds until the asparagus is cool enough to handle.

2. Preheat the grill to high.

3. Oil a shallow ovenproof platter, then arrange the warm asparagus on top in a neat row and in a single layer (see tip). Drizzle over a little olive oil, season with salt and pepper and scatter the Parmesan evenly across the middle of the asparagus spears.

4. Slide under the grill to cook for 3–5 minutes or until the cheese has melted and is golden and bubbling.

5. To make the dip, mix all the ingredients together and season with salt and pepper.

6. Serve the asparagus hot with the garlic dip and granary bread.

Mary's Classic Tips:
* The easiest way to prepare asparagus is to bend the stalks so that they snap – they will break just above the unwanted woody ends.
* If the asparagus is too soft and bendy it is difficult to dip, so err on the undercooked side to ensure that it stays rigid.
* It's important to lay the asparagus in a single layer so that the cheese is evenly distributed. If you don't have an ovenproof platter that is large enough to cook the asparagus in a single layer, grill in two batches instead.

Parmesan Melba Toasts

MAKES **16 toasts** / COOK TIME: **8–10 minutes**

2 medium slices of
   white bread
Olive oil, for brushing
25g (1oz) Parmesan cheese,
   finely grated
Salt and freshly ground
   black pepper

Prepare Ahead:
Can be made up to 4 hours
ahead and kept in an
airtight container.

Perfect served with soup or pâté. Thin, crisp and curled, just as they should be, with the added bonus of cheesy Parmesan.

1. Preheat the oven to 200°C/180°C fan/Gas 6.

2. Toast the bread on both sides until lightly golden brown. Cut off the crusts while still warm (see tip) and slice the toast in half horizontally through the middle to make four very thin slices in total. Leave to cool a little.

3. Brush the cut side of each slice of toast with olive oil. Season with salt and pepper and sprinkle with the Parmesan cheese.

4. Slice each piece diagonally into four triangles. Place on a baking sheet and bake in the oven for 8–10 minutes or until golden and the edges have curled up. Remove from the oven and leave to cool.

Mary's Classic Tip:
* Even small amounts of discarded crusts are worth saving for making into breadcrumbs. Whizz in a food processor and freeze the crumbs in a resealable bag. Add to them every time you have leftover crusts so you always have breadcrumbs on hand. Great for topping fish fillets or pasta dishes for extra crunch.

Parma Ham & Courgette Bites

MAKES 20 canapés

1 large courgette, ends
    trimmed
5 slices of Parma ham
2–3 tbsp sun-dried
    tomato paste
100g (4oz) unripe soft goat's
    cheese with a rind, chopped
    into 20 small cubes
20 small basil leaves

Prepare Ahead:
These can be prepared
8 hours in advance and kept
in the fridge until ready to
serve.

Mary's Classic Tip:
* A Y-shaped vegetable
    peeler gives the best results
    for courgette ribbons. Hold
    the courgette flat on the
    chopping board, press
    down hard with the peeler
    and pull it down the length
    of the courgette to give
    lovely thin, even pieces.

These are really tasty morsels; the salty ham, sharp cheese and sweet-tasting tomato purée make the perfect combination all in one mouthful.

1. Cut the courgette in half across the middle so you have two pieces each about 9cm (3½in) long. Using a vegetable peeler, peel thin ribbons of courgette to make 20 good-sized strips in total. (You will be able to cut plenty, so choose the best – see tip.)

2. Bring a pan of salted water to the boil and blanch the courgette ribbons for 10–15 seconds until just softened, bendy and almost translucent. Lift out with a slotted spoon and transfer to a bowl of cold water, then drain and lay on a board lined with kitchen paper to dry. You may want to do this in batches to make sure you don't overcrowd the pan and the water continues to boil.

3. Lay a slice of Parma ham on a board, taking care as it tears easily. Place four courgette ribbons on top, laying them side by side and with a slight gap between each strip.

4. Using a sharp knife, slice in between the courgette ribbons and through the Parma ham to make four single strips. Then turn over so that the courgette is underneath and the ham on top. Put a small blob of sun-dried tomato paste on the ham, at the bottom of each strip. Place a basil leaf on top, then a cube of cheese. Roll up tightly to make a small cylinder shape with the courgette now on the outside.

5. Repeat with the remaining ingredients to make 20 canapés, then chill in the fridge until ready to eat.

Step-by-step images overleaf →

Making the Parma Ham & Courgette Bites:

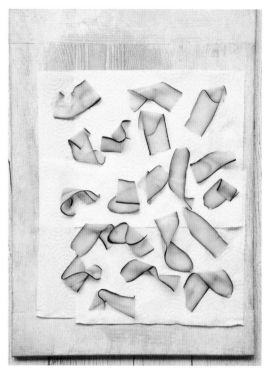

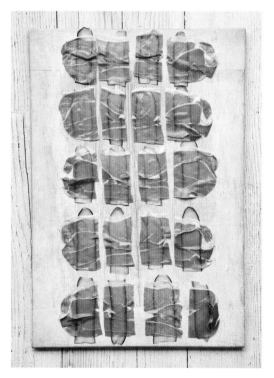

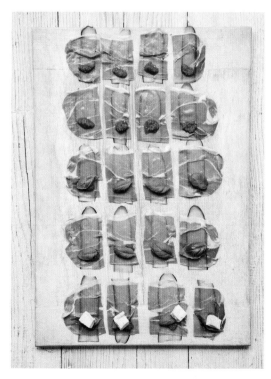

French Onion Soup with Mustard Cheese Croûtes

SERVES 6–8 / COOK TIME: 40–45 minutes

50g (2oz) butter
1 tbsp olive oil
6 large white onions, thinly
    sliced (see tip)
1½ tbsp caster sugar
200ml (7fl oz) white wine
2 litres (3½ pints) rich beef
    stock or vegetable stock
    (see tip)
3 bay leaves
1 sprig of rosemary
Salt and freshly ground
    black pepper

For the croûtes
½ thin baguette
Dijon mustard, for spreading
25g (1oz) Gruyère cheese,
    grated

Prepare Ahead:
The soup can be made up
to 4 days ahead. The
croûtes can be assembled up
to 8 hours ahead, then
finished under the grill just
before serving.

Freeze:
The soup freezes well.

Classic and delicious, no modern twist needed. The cheesy croûtes have a nice mustard hit to them.

1. Heat the butter and oil in a deep saucepan. When the butter has melted, add the onions and fry over a high heat for about 2–3 minutes. Lower the heat, cover with a lid and cook for about 10 minutes or until starting to soften.

2. Remove the lid, sprinkle in the sugar and season with salt and pepper, then fry over a high heat for 2–3 minutes, stirring. Reduce the heat to low and cook for 15 minutes, stirring occasionally, until the onions are tender, golden and caramelised.

3. Preheat the grill to medium-high.

4. Pour in the wine and boil for 2-3 minutes to allow the alcohol to evaporate. Add the stock and herbs, then bring back up to the boil and simmer over a medium-high heat for 8–10 minutes.

5. Meanwhile, make the croûtes. Slice the baguette into 6 thick or 12 thinner slices and toast one side under the grill. Spread the untoasted side with mustard and top with cheese. Pop under the grill for a few minutes to cook until just melted.

6. Remove the herbs from the soup, check the seasoning and serve in warmed bowls with the mustard cheese croûtes on top.

Mary's Classic Tips:
* Leave the root on when slicing the onions. It holds the onion together and helps to reduce the inevitable tears!
* A homemade stock or fresh stock from the supermarket give the best flavour for this dish; if not, a concentrated stock pot would be preferable to a powdered cube. Beef stock is traditional but vegetable stock can be substituted for vegetarians.

Celeriac & Watercress Soup

SERVES 6 / COOK TIME: 25–35 minutes

2 tbsp sunflower oil

2 large onions,
roughly chopped

750g (1lb 10oz) peeled
celeriac, diced

1½ litres (2½ pints) vegetable
or chicken stock

200g (7oz) watercress,
reserving a few sprigs
to garnish

About 4 tbsp full-fat crème
fraîche or double cream

Salt and freshly ground
black pepper

I am a soup addict, my lunchtime staple all year round in fact. Avoid keeping the soup hot on the hob as the watercress will lose its vibrant green colour. If a little on the thick slide, slacken with stock. Adding the celeriac to the watercress makes this lovely soup a bit more substantial and filling.

1. Heat the oil in a large deep saucepan. Add the onion and fry over a medium heat for 5 minutes until just starting to brown. Add the celeriac and fry for 4–5 minutes, stirring occasionally, until starting to colour. Pour in the stock and season with salt and pepper.

2. Cover with a lid and bring to the boil, then reduce the heat and simmer for 15–20 minutes until completely tender.

3. Add the watercress and stir over the heat for 2–3 minutes until wilted. Blend until smooth, either with a hand blender or in a free-standing blender or food processor (see tip). Swirl through the crème fraîche or double cream and check the seasoning.

4. Serve piping hot with the reserved watercress sprigs and a fresh muffin (see page 261).

Mary's Classic Tips:

* If you have any leftover celeriac, use it in Masses of Mash on page 177.
* If using a free-standing blender or food processor to blend, reheat the soup before serving as it will cool down in the machine.

Lentil & Sweet Potato Soup

SERVES 6–8 / COOK TIME: 25 minutes

2 tbsp olive oil
1 onion, sliced
2 carrots, peeled and diced
1 red pepper, deseeded
    and diced
200g (7oz) sweet potatoes,
    peeled and diced
2 garlic cloves, crushed
2 tbsp tomato purée
1 x 400g tin of green lentils,
    drained and rinsed
1.1 litres (2 pints) vegetable
    stock (see tip)
½ tsp sugar
Salt and freshly ground
    black pepper
1 tbsp chopped parsley,
    to garnish

....

Prepare Ahead:
Can be made up to 3 days
ahead and reheated to serve.

....

Freeze:
Freezes well.

Lentil soup is classic; adding sweet potato instead of white potatoes gives a stronger flavour. The sweet potato adds to the rich orange colour as well as giving a more intense flavour – perfect warming soup for a winter's day.

1. Heat the oil in a large deep saucepan, add the onion, carrots, red pepper and sweet potatoes and fry for over a high heat, stirring, for 3–4 minutes. Add the garlic and tomato purée and cook for another 30 seconds.

2. Add the lentils and stock, season with salt and pepper and a pinch of sugar, stir and bring to the boil. Lower the heat, then cover with a lid and simmer for about 20 minutes or until the vegetables have softened.

3. Blend until smooth, either with a hand blender or in a free-standing blender or food processor. Taste to check the seasoning.

4. Serve piping hot in warmed bowls, sprinkled with parsley, and with some crusty bread on the side.

Mary's Classic Tips:
∗ Add less stock for a thicker, creamier consistency if preferred.
∗ If you prefer, use beef or chicken stock.

Spinach, Pea & Blue Cheese Soup

SERVES 6 / COOK TIME: 15–25 minutes

A knob of butter

2 bunches of spring
onions, sliced

3 celery sticks, sliced

250g (9oz) potatoes,
peeled and cut into 2cm
(¾in) cubes

1.2 litres (2 pints 2fl oz)
vegetable stock (see tip)

500g (1lb 2oz) frozen petit
pois, defrosted

225g (8oz) baby spinach

75g (3oz) Stilton cheese,
grated

Salt and freshly ground
black pepper

50ml (2fl oz) double cream,
to serve (optional)

Prepare Ahead:
Can be made up to a
day ahead.

Freeze:
Freezes well.

Spinach and blue cheese is such a classic soup. I like the addition of peas as this gives a depth of flavour and bright green colour to the soup. A lovely soup with a mild flavour of the blue cheese – it could take a little more if you like the taste.

1. Melt the butter in a large saucepan. Add the spring onions and celery and fry over a medium heat for 2–3 minutes, then stir in the potatoes and add the stock. Cover with a lid and bring to the boil, then reduce the heat and simmer for 10–15 minutes until the potatoes are soft.

2. Add the peas and spinach and simmer for about 4 minutes until soft. Check the seasoning and add salt and pepper to taste.

3. Blend until smooth, either with a hand blender or in a free-standing blender or food processor. Add the grated cheese and stir until melted. Spoon into individual bowls and drizzle with a little double cream, if you like (see tip).

Mary's Classic Tips:
* A sprinkling of snipped chives would also go well with this soup.
* If you prefer, use beef or chicken stock.

Prawn Croûtes

MAKES **20 croûtes** / COOK TIME: **18–20 minutes**

1 small thin baguette
3 tbsp olive oil
4 tbsp full-fat mayonnaise
1 tsp tomato purée
A few drops of
    Worcestershire sauce
A squeeze of lemon juice
1 tbsp hot horseradish sauce
1 tsp chopped parsley
200g (7oz) small peeled
    North Atlantic cooked
    prawns, patted dry
Paprika, for sprinkling
Salt and freshly ground
    black pepper

....

Prepare Ahead:
Can be assembled up to
5 hours ahead. The croûtes
can be baked in the oven and
stored in an airtight container
for 2–3 days before topping.

Savoury-tasting prawns on crisp toasts – perfect to pop straight in your mouth with one hand while holding a chilled glass of wine in the other!

1. Preheat the oven to 200°C/180°C fan/Gas 6.

2. Slice the baguette into 20 slices around 1cm (½in) thick. Brush the slices with olive oil on both sides and place on a baking sheet. Bake in the oven for about 10 minutes until crispy and golden brown.

3. In a small bowl, mix together the mayonnaise, tomato purée, Worcestershire sauce, lemon juice, horseradish sauce and parsley. Add the prawns and season with salt and pepper. Mix together well, then spoon on top of the croûtes and sprinkle with paprika.

4. Put back in the oven to bake for another 8–10 minutes until lightly golden. Serve warm.

Mary's Classic Tip:
* Even though I much prefer large prawns, on this occasion tiny prawns are perfect for the recipe. Brown shrimps would work well too.

Eggs Benedict with Spinach

SERVES 4 / COOK TIME: 15–25 minutes

8 thin rashers of streaky bacon

Butter, for spreading
and frying

4 eggs

2 English muffins (to make
your own, see page 261),
sliced in half

200g (7oz) baby spinach

For the hollandaise sauce

2 egg yolks

1 tsp white wine vinegar, plus
extra for poaching the eggs

100g (4oz) unsalted butter,
melted

Salt and freshly ground
black pepper

....

Prepare Ahead:
The hollandaise sauce can be
made up to an hour ahead
and kept warm in a wide-
necked vacuum flask.

**A classic dish, such a treat to have when eating out but thought
to be tricky at home – it needs care but is well worthwhile, have
a go! Use smoked bacon if liked.**

1. Fry the bacon for 4–5 minutes until crisp, in a dry, nonstick
   frying pan over a high heat or under the grill, then set aside
   to keep warm.

2. To make the hollandaise sauce, use a hand whisk to whisk
   the yolks and vinegar together in a medium bowl until
   blended (see tip). Set the bowl over a saucepan of gently
   simmering water. Gradually pour in the melted butter in
   a thin stream, whisking continuously over the heat, until
   the sauce has thickened and become glossy. Season with
   salt and pepper, then remove from the heat, cover the bowl
   with cling film and set aside.

3. Bring the same pan up to the boil, adding more water if
   needed – enough to poach the eggs. Reduce the heat to a
   simmer and add a dash of vinegar to the water. Crack each
   egg into a ramekin or cup, swirl the water with a spoon and
   then carefully drop into the pan. Leave until the white is just
   beginning to set and carefully turn with a slotted spoon to
   form into an oval shape (see tip).

Continued overleaf →

4. Simmer for 3–4 minutes or until the white is set and the yolk is soft in the middle. Keep an eye on the heat: if the water starts to bubble again, turn it down to stop it disrupting the egg's shape. Using a slotted spoon, carefully lift out and drain on kitchen paper.

5. Toast and butter the muffins and arrange on four plates.

6. Melt a knob of butter in a frying pan and briefly fry the spinach until wilted, then season with salt and pepper.

7. Spoon some spinach on top of each muffin half, top with an egg and a spoonful of hollandaise and arrange two bacon rashers in a cross on top. Serve hot.

Mary's Classic Tips:
* Using a hand whisk for making the hollandaise sauce gives better control over the final texture – you don't want it to be whipped and become too thick to pour.
* Don't panic when first tipping an egg into the poaching water. The egg white will naturally spread out, but it comes together as it cooks, and you can tidy the edges at the end when the cooked egg is draining on kitchen paper.

Smoked Salmon on Rye with Dill Pickle

SERVES 6

3 slices of light rye bread
3 tbsp full-fat mayonnaise
1½ tsp Dijon mustard
6 large slices of smoked
  salmon (see tip)
30g (1oz) pickled cucumber
  spears with dill (from a
  jar), sliced into tiny pieces
1 tbsp finely snipped chives
Salt and freshly ground
  black pepper
Rocket leaves or watercress,
  to serve

....

Prepare Ahead:
Can be assembled up to
3 hours ahead.

This is great for a first course, or you can cut each piece into three to serve as a canapé. Rye bread is a dense, dark flavoursome bread with a firm texture, which can now be found in most good supermarkets. Any slices not used can be frozen for another occasion.

1. Cut each slice of bread in half, giving six long rectangles.

2. Mix the mayonnaise and mustard together, season with salt and pepper and spread over the bread.

3. Thinly slice the smoked salmon into short strips and scatter over the mayonnaise. Arrange the tiny pieces of pickled cucumber on top and sprinkle with the chives.

4. Serve one salmon-topped slice of bread per person with a few rocket leaves or watercress to decorate

Mary's Classic Tips:
* Choose wild smoked salmon, if available, as it is usually better quality than farmed smoked salmon, with a good firm texture for slicing finely.
* Buy the rye bread in cellophane packets already sliced.

Prawn Cocktail

SERVES 6

350g (12oz) small peeled
   North Atlantic cooked
   prawns, patted dry
½ large iceberg lettuce,
   shredded
12 large unpeeled cooked
   prawns, heads removed
6 sprigs of parsley
6 lemon wedges
Paprika, for sprinkling

For the sauce
150ml (5fl oz) full-fat
   mayonnaise
2 tsp sun-dried tomato paste
1 tsp Worcestershire sauce
1 tbsp hot horseradish sauce
A squeeze of lemon juice,
   to taste
Salt and freshly ground
   black pepper

....

Prepare Ahead:
Can be made and assembled
up to 6 hours ahead, then
kept in the fridge until needed.

Classic, retro it has had all the names, but a prawn cocktail is a delicious first course that will never be forgotten. Quick to assemble and a tasty starter, it is straightforward and can be assembled well ahead of time. The rich dressing has a subtle piquancy from the horseradish sauce and is made from easy, store-cupboard ingredients.

1. You will need six dessert glasses or wine glasses.

2. Make the sauce by measuring the mayonnaise, tomato paste, Worcestershire sauce, horseradish sauce and lemon juice into a large bowl. Season with salt and pepper and mix together well before stirring in the small peeled prawns.

3. Season the lettuce and divide between the glasses.

4. Spoon the mixed prawns and sauce on top of the lettuce in each glass. Arrange two large prawns on top of the sauce, add a sprig of parsley and slide a lemon wedge on to the rim of the glass.

5. Sprinkle with paprika just before serving and serve with buttered brown bread.

Mary's Classic Tip:
* This is where iceberg lettuce is best to use, as it stays lovely
   and crisp and does not wilt.

Smoked Salmon & Avocado Terrines

MAKES 6 terrines / CHILLING TIME: A minimum of 2 hours

300g (11oz) smoked
    salmon slices
1 banana shallot, finely diced
1 large just-ripe avocado,
    peeled and diced into 1cm
    (½in) chunks
2 medium tomatoes, skinned
    (see tip), deseeded and cut
    into chunks
¼ tsp finely chopped and
    deseeded red chilli
4 tbsp chopped dill
3 tbsp full-fat cream cheese
Juice of ½ lemon
Salt and freshly ground
    black pepper
Rocket leaves, to serve

Prepare Ahead:
Can be made up to a
day ahead.

**A classic flavour combination and ideal for a prepare ahead
cold starter or light lunch. Easy to exchange ingredients
depending on what is in the fridge: swap dill for chives,
shallot for a little red onion, etc.**

1. You will need six ramekins (see tip). Line each of these
   with cling film, leaving plenty overhanging the edges,
   to fold over the top of the terrines later.

2. Use the smoked salmon slices to neatly line each of the
   ramekins until the base and sides are completely covered.
   Don't worry if the smoked salmon comes over the sides;
   it will be tucked in later.

3. Place all the remaining ingredients (except the rocket) in
   a bowl, season with salt and pepper and stir to combine.
   Divide the mixture among the salmon-lined ramekins
   and level the tops with the back of a spoon. Fold over any
   overhanging salmon, cover with cling film and carefully
   press down. Chill in the fridge for a minimum of 2 hours.

4. Arrange some rocket leaves on each plate. Turn out each
   terrine, remove the cling film and sit on top of the rocket.
   Serve with sourdough bread.

Mary's Classic Tips:
* To skin tomatoes, cut a cross in the top of each tomato, place
  in a bowl and cover with boiling water. Leave to stand for a
  couple of minutes, then drain and rinse in cold water. The
  skins will now peel off easily.
* If you don't have six ramekins, you could use any small dishes,
  glasses or small coffee cups for this – anything with straight
  sides will work well.

Beetroot Gravadlax

SERVES 10 / CHILLING TIME: 24 hours (to cure the salmon)

1kg (2lb 3oz) side of salmon
   fillet, skin on
150g (5oz) raw beetroot,
   peeled and grated
50g (2oz) demerara sugar
50g (2oz) sea salt flakes
1 tsp black peppercorns,
   freshly ground

For the sauce
100g (4oz) pickled cucumber
   spears with dill (from a
   jar), finely diced
2 rounded tbsp hot
   horseradish sauce
150ml (5fl oz) soured cream
2 tbsp chopped parsley
Salt and freshly ground
   black pepper

For the salad
50g (2oz) pea shoots
50g (2oz) raw beetroot,
   peeled and very finely
   shredded into thin strips
50g (2oz) pickled cucumber
   spears with dill, very
   finely diced

Prepare Ahead:
Can be made up to
4 days ahead.

Freeze:
Freezes well, for up
to 6 weeks.

Gravadlax is one of my most favourite first courses – the addition of grated beetroot gives a wonderful colour and flavour too. I use some of the leftovers to make the little salmon and avocado terrines, which look pretty with the pink edging.

1. Put the salmon fillet, skin side down, in the middle of a large piece of foil – at least double the size of the fish.

2. Mix the beetroot, sugar, salt and pepper in a bowl. Spread over the surface of the salmon and press down firmly. Wrap the salmon in the foil and scrunch up the open edges to make a sealed parcel.

3. Place on a large tray, put a small roasting tin on top and add some weights or unopened tins to weigh the fish down (see tip). Place in the fridge to cure for 24 hours.

4. Mix all of the sauce ingredients together in a small bowl and season well with salt and pepper.

5. When ready to serve, drain off the liquid from the foil parcel, then scrape off the grated beetroot topping from the salmon. Slice the gravadlax (see tip) and arrange a few slices on each plate. Place a few pea shoots by the salmon and scatter some of the beetroot and pickled cucumber pieces on top of the pea shoots. Spoon a little of the sauce next to the salad.

Mary's Classic Tips:
* If you can't find a tray large enough for the salmon, use the grill pan or a roasting tin. It needs to have an edge or lip, though, as plenty of ruby red juice will leak out during the cure and needs containing.
* To carve the salmon, use a long, sharp knife. Long and steady strokes cut on the diagonal will give the best slices for presentation, a little thicker than salmon is usually sliced, holding the knife at a gentle 5–10-degree angle.

FISH

Dover Sole with Lemon Butter

SERVES 2 / COOK TIME: 6–8 minutes

2 Dover soles, heads on or
off and both sides skinned
(see tip)
20–25g (¾–1oz) butter,
softened
Salt and freshly ground
black pepper

For the lemon butter
50g (2oz) butter, softened
1 tbsp chopped parsley
Juice of 1 lemon, plus extra
to serve

....

Prepare Ahead:
The lemon butter can be
mixed up to a week ahead
and kept in the fridge.

**The King of the Sea, Dover sole is such a treat, expensive but
well worth it for its delicate taste. Do not try and cook too many at
once or they will overcook. A lovely fish with a classic treatment.**

1. Lay the fish on a board. Trim the fins using a sharp pair of
   scissors (see tip), then season well with salt and pepper and
   spread one side with half the softened butter.

2. To make the lemon butter, add the butter, parsley and lemon
   juice to a bowl. Season well with salt and pepper and mix
   together until combined.

3. Heat a large griddle or frying pan until hot. Fry one of the
   fish on the buttered side over a medium-high heat for about
   1–2 minutes until sealed and lightly golden. Spread the
   remaining butter on top and sprinkle with salt and pepper,
   then carefully flip over using a fish slice. Fry for a further
   2 minutes and transfer to a serving dish or baking tray and
   keep warm. Repeat for the second Dover sole. With a very
   large frying pan you will be able to cook both side by side.

4. Heat the lemon butter in the hot pan until just melted and
   then pour over both fish. Squeeze over more lemon to serve.

5. Either present the fish as they are or carefully cut the top two
   fillets from the bone and gently remove to serve.

Mary's Classic Tips:
* Ask your fishmonger to skin the soles for you. To do it yourself,
  lay the fish with the brown skin on top. Make a sharp incision
  across the skin just above the tail and start to ease the skin off
  with a knife. Once it is loose enough to hold, pull the skin off in
  one piece, using a tea towel to help you grip. Flip the fish over
  and remove the underbelly skin in the same way.
* Make sure you trim the fins for a more professional finish,
  otherwise they stick to the pan and become mixed in the
  lemon butter.

Kedgeree

SERVES 4–6 / COOK TIME: 30 minutes

400g (14oz) undyed smoked
   haddock fillet, skin on
30g (1oz) butter
2 tbsp olive oil
1 onion, chopped
300g (11oz) basmati rice
1 tbsp curry powder
1 tsp ground turmeric
500–600ml (18fl oz–1 pint)
   vegetable stock
150g (5oz) button
   mushrooms, sliced
Juice of 1 small lemon
4 tbsp double cream
Salt and freshly ground
   black pepper

To garnish
1 large onion, sliced thinly
3 eggs
½ small bunch of coriander,
   chopped

One of my absolute favourite dishes and a really tasty combination of flavours – the fried onion topping and soft-boiled egg complement the smoky fish and spiced rice. Check halfway through cooking and if a little dry, add more stock. For more crunch and extra flavour, add a topping of about 25g toasted flaked almonds.

1. Preheat the oven to 200°C/180°C fan/Gas 6.

2. Lay a piece of foil on a baking sheet. Sit the haddock, skin side down, on top and place half the butter on top of the fish. Season with pepper and a little salt, then fold in the sides of the foil to make a parcel, scrunching together the open edges to seal.

3. Bake for 15–18 minutes or until the fish is cooked. It should be opaque and flake easily. Peel off the skin, removing and discarding any obvious bones, and set aside, keeping it wrapped in foil so it stays warm and holds the juices.

4. Meanwhile, pour half the oil into a large frying pan over a high heat. Add the onion and fry for 2–4 minutes. Add the rice, curry powder and turmeric and stir together for about a minute, so that the rice is coated in the spices.

5. Pour in 500ml (18fl oz) of the stock, cover with a lid and bring to the boil. Allow to boil for 2 minutes, then reduce the heat and simmer very gently for 12–15 minutes, adding more stock if needed, or until all of the liquid has been absorbed and the rice is just cooked but still with a slight bite. Remove from the heat and set aside with the lid on while you finish making the kedgeree.

6. While the rice is cooking, prepare the garnish. Pour the remaining oil into another frying pan, add the sliced onion and fry over a medium heat for about 10 minutes until soft and golden, then tip on to a plate and set aside.

Continued overleaf →

7. Place the eggs in a saucepan, cover with cold water and bring to the boil. Cook for 4–5 minutes or until soft-boiled, then plunge immediately into cold water to stop the eggs cooking further. Carefully peel away the shell and cut into quarters (see tip).

8. Wipe out the pan used for cooking the onion, add the rest of the butter and melt over a high heat. Add the mushrooms and fry for about 4 minutes until browned.

9. Tip the fried mushrooms into the cooked rice with the lemon juice and cream and mix together carefully, so that the mushrooms are evenly distributed. Add the haddock with all of its buttery juices to the rice and gently fold in. Use a spatula, allowing the fish to flake but keeping a few distinct pieces, and mix everything together, seasoning with salt and pepper to taste.

10. Spoon the kedgeree into a warmed serving dish and garnish with the golden sliced onion, chopped coriander and soft-boiled eggs.

Mary's Classic Tips:
* Soft-boiled eggs are delicious, if tricky to peel! The secret is to use week-old eggs rather than ultra-fresh ones. Plunging into cold water after boiling is also important – it stops the egg from overcooking, prevents a black ring from forming around the yolk and helps loosen the shell.
* To peel a boiled egg, tap gently round the shell and roll it gently in your hands to help to loosen the white from the membrane. Peel with your fingers or use a spoon to help ease the shell off. Keeping an egg in water while peeling can also help.

Bouillabaisse

SERVES 6 / COOK TIME: 55 minutes

2 tbsp olive oil
2 onions, finely chopped
1 small fennel bulb, trimmed
    and finely diced
2 garlic cloves, crushed
1 rounded tbsp tomato purée
100ml (3½fl oz) white wine
750ml (1 pint 6fl oz) fish stock
6 large tomatoes, skinned
    (see tip on page 40),
    deseeded and chopped
A good pinch of
    saffron strands
1 small bunch of basil,
    stalks tied together and
    leaves shredded
Finely grated zest of 1 small
    orange and juice of ½ orange
1kg (2lb 3oz) mussels, cleaned
    and debearded (see tip)
2 sea bass fillets, skinned and
    cut into 5 slices
350g (12oz) cod, skinned
    and cut into slices 1.5cm
    (⅝in) thick
200g (7oz) peeled
    cooked crayfish tails,
    shells removed
Salt and freshly ground
    black pepper

For the rouille
6 rounded tbsp full-fat
    mayonnaise
1 large garlic clove, crushed
A pinch of saffron strands
    soaked in the juice of
    ½ small lemon

Rich and tasty bouillabaisse was originally a fish stew made by Marseilles fishermen using the bony rockfish that they were unable to sell to restaurants or markets. We now add the fish of our choice, but using traditional flavours and serving it with a rouille make this a classic bouillabaisse recipe. Try to find sustainable fish.

1. Heat the oil in a large, deep saucepan. Add the onions and fennel and sauté over a medium heat for 5 minutes until starting to soften. Add the garlic and tomato purée and stir for 30 seconds. Pour in the wine and stock and add the tomatoes. Bring to the boil, then add the saffron, basil stalks and orange zest, cover with a lid and simmer for 10 minutes.

2. Add the mussels and stir them into the pan. Cover again with the lid, bring back up to the boil and cook for about 4 minutes until all of the mussels have opened. Take the pan off the heat and use a slotted spoon to carefully scoop the cooked mussels in their shells into a bowl, making sure you haven't left any in the pan. Leave to cool for a few minutes while you blend the soup.

3. Discard the basil stalks and blend the soup until completely smooth – this is easiest with a hand blender. Simmer the soup, uncovered, for 10 minutes to reduce (you should have about 2 litres/2 pints 2fl oz in total at this point).

4. Meanwhile, make the rouille. Mix all the ingredients together in a small bowl, season with salt and pepper and set aside.

Continued overleaf →

5. When the mussels are cool enough to handle, reserve 18 mussels in their shells, then remove the remaining mussels from their shells and place in another small bowl.

6. Season the soup with salt and pepper and add the orange juice. Add the sea bass and cod, cover again and gently simmer for 3–4 minutes, then add the cooked mussels, the reserved mussels in their shells and the crayfish tails and simmer for another 2–3 minutes until heated through and all of the fish is cooked.

7. Divide the bouillabaisse among bowls, spoon some of the rouille into each bowl, sprinkle with the shredded basil leaves and serve.

Mary's Classic Tip:
* Give the mussels a good scrub and a couple of rinses before cooking as the shells are an integral part of the sauce and you want as little grit in there as possible. Discard any shells that remain open when tapped and, once cooked, discard any that remained closed and didn't open in the stew.

Moules Marinière

SERVES 2 as a main dish or 4 as a starter / COOK TIME: 20 minutes

2 tbsp oil
2 large banana shallots,
    finely chopped
4 garlic cloves, crushed
175ml (6fl oz) white wine
1kg (2lb 3oz) mussels,
    cleaned and debearded
    (see tip on page 52)
150ml (5fl oz) double cream
Juice of ½ lemon
Salt and freshly ground
    black pepper
1 bunch of parsley,
    chopped, to serve

The most popular recipe for mussels and one of my go-to favourites. It's essential that every mussel is tightly closed before cooking them.

1. Heat the oil in a large pan, add the shallots and fry over medium heat for 3–4 minutes. Add the garlic and fry for a further 30 seconds. Add the wine and mussels, stirring to combine and seasoning with a little salt and pepper. Bring to the boil, then cover with a lid and cook for 3–4 minutes until all the mussels have opened. (Discard any mussels that remain closed.)

2. Spoon the mussels into a bowl using a slotted spoon, leaving all the liquid in the pan. Boil the cooking liquid for about 3 minutes until it is reduced by half. (You should end up with about 150ml/5fl oz of liquid.) Add the cream and boil again for a few minutes. Check the seasoning, then add the lemon juice and return the mussels to the pan.

3. Toss the mussels in the liquid and sprinkle with the chopped parsley. Serve in a large warmed bowl with some crusty bread to mop up the sauce (see tip).

Mary's Classic Tip:
* Don't forget to serve the mussels with finger bowls and also a bowl for the empty mussel shells.

Sea Bass Steaks with Lentils & Rosemary

SERVES 6 / COOK TIME: 50–55 minutes

6 sea bass steaks
   (see tip), skinned
2 tbsp chopped
   rosemary leaves
2 tbsp olive oil
A knob of butter

For the lentils
2 tbsp olive oil
4 celery sticks, very finely diced
1 large onion, very finely diced
1 carrot, very finely diced
½ red pepper, deseeded and
   very finely diced
¼ fresh red chilli, deseeded
   and finely diced
2 garlic cloves, crushed
150g (5oz) dried Puy lentils,
   rinsed (see tip)
150 (5oz) dried red split
   lentils, rinsed (see tip)
200ml (7fl oz) white wine
600ml (1 pint) vegetable stock
1 tbsp finely chopped
   rosemary leaves
3 tbsp full-fat crème fraîche
A squeeze of lemon juice
2 tbsp sun-dried tomato paste
4 tbsp finely chopped parsley
Salt and freshly ground
   black pepper

Prepare Ahead:
Cook the lentils up to
8 hours ahead. The fish can
be prepared up to 4 hours
ahead, ready to bake.

Hearty, healthy and bursting with flavour. A warming dish, full of goodness. Use whichever fish your family like best.

1. Preheat the oven to 200°C/180°C fan/Gas 6.

2. First cook the lentils. Heat the oil in large, wide saucepan or sauté pan. Add the celery, onion, carrot and red pepper and fry over a high heat for about 5 minutes until they are starting to brown. Add the chilli and garlic, then add all the lentils and stir to coat in the mixture.

3. Pour in the wine and stock and bring to the boil, stirring. Add the rosemary and cover with a lid, then reduce the heat and simmer for 30–35 minutes or until tender and the liquid has been absorbed.

4. Stir in the crème fraîche, lemon juice, tomato paste and parsley. Season, then remove from the hob and keep warm.

5. Season the sea bass with salt and pepper and press the chopped rosemary into the fish. Heat the oil and butter in a frying pan and, when the butter has melted, cook the fish over a medium heat for about 2 minutes on each side or until sealed.

6. Transfer to a roasting tin into which all six pieces of fish will neatly fit. Pour over any buttery juices from the pan and bake in the oven for about 10 minutes or until cooked through.

7. Spoon the lentils on to each plate, add a sea bass steak and serve piping hot.

Mary's Classic Tips:
* If you can't find sea bass steaks, you could use fillets instead and simply pan-fry for 2–3 minutes on each side (no need to then bake them in the oven).
* There is no need to soak the lentils before cooking; just give them a little rinse before adding to the pan. And avoid adding salt during cooking as it can make them tough.

Plaice Topped with Spinach & Mushrooms

SERVES 6 / COOK TIME: 15–19 minutes, plus cooling and resting

6 plaice fillets (150–175g/5–6oz each), skinned (see tip)

Paprika, for sprinkling

For the topping
230g (8oz) baby spinach
1 tbsp olive oil
250g (9oz) chestnut mushrooms, cut into 1cm (½in) dice
2 tbsp full-fat cream cheese
75g (3oz) Gruyère cheese, grated
Salt and freshly ground black pepper

Prepare Ahead:
The topping can be prepared up to 8 hours in advance.

An easy dish to prepare, which is great for a quick evening supper, but just as good for entertaining. You can make in advance and it looks impressive and is quick to cook.

1. Preheat the oven to 200°C/180°C fan/Gas 6 and line one or two baking trays with baking paper.

2. First make the topping. Put the spinach in a colander and pour over a kettle of boiling water to wilt the leaves. Leave to cool, then squeeze out all of the liquid. Season with salt and black pepper.

3. Heat a frying pan until hot. Add the oil and mushrooms and fry over a high heat for 3–4 minutes until cooked and lightly golden. Leave to cool and then drain away any excess juices.

4. Add the mushrooms to a bowl with the cream cheese and half the Gruyère. Mix together and season.

5. Season the lined baking trays with salt and pepper. Lay the plaice fillets on top and season again. Divide the cold mushroom mixture among the fillets, then top each with a layer of spinach and the remaining cheese. Sprinkle with a dusting of paprika.

6. Bake in the oven for 12–15 minutes until lightly golden and the fish is cooked through. Leave to rest for 5 minutes, covered in foil, then serve with new potatoes and green beans.

Mary's Classic Tip:
* Ask your fishmonger for fillets of a similar size and to skin the fillets for you. To skin flatfish yourself, see tip on page 45.

Spiced Sea Bream Pilaf

SERVES 6 / MARINATE: A minimum of 15 minutes / COOK TIME: 35 minutes

750g (1¾lb) skinned sea
  bream or sea bass fillets,
  cut into 3cm (1¼in) pieces
1 tsp curry powder
½ tsp ground cumin
½ tsp ground coriander
Juice of ½ lemon
2 tbsp olive oil
A knob of butter
Salt and freshly ground
  black pepper
1 bunch of coriander,
  chopped, to serve

For the pilaf
2 tbsp olive oil
2 onions, chopped
2 garlic cloves, crushed
200g (7oz) chestnut
  mushrooms, sliced
300g (11oz) long-grain
  white rice
1 tbsp curry powder
½ tsp ground turmeric
500ml (18fl oz) vegetable
  or fish stock
75g (3oz) peas (fresh or frozen)
3 tbsp mango chutney
4 tbsp soy sauce
Juice of ½ lemon

Prepare Ahead:
The rice can be made up
to 4 hours ahead.

The versatile sea bream goes well with this lightly curried pilaf. The pilaf has a really intense savoury flavour and the soy makes the rice quite dark and salty, but the chutney sweetens it. This dish would work equally well with chicken.

1. Place the fish pieces in a bowl, add the spices, salt and pepper and lemon juice, toss to coat and leave to marinate in the fridge for at least 15 minutes while you cook the rice.

2. Preheat the oven 200°C/180°C fan/Gas 6.

3. Heat the oil in a flameproof and ovenproof casserole dish or ovenproof frying pan. Add the onions and garlic and fry over a high heat for about 2 minutes, then tip in the mushrooms and fry for another minute. Add the rice and spices, season with salt and pepper and fry for 1 minute, stirring. Pour in the stock, bring to the boil and transfer to the oven to cook (without a lid) for about 30 minutes or until the rice is tender and all the liquid has been absorbed.

4. A few minutes before the rice is ready, cook the fish, first draining it of excess marinade so that it fries rather than stews. Heat the oil in a large frying pan, add the butter and, when it has melted, fry the fish over a high heat for about 4 minutes, turning, until cooked through. You may have to do this in batches.

5. Cook the peas for 5 minutes in boiling salted water (see tip), then stir into the rice with the chutney, soy sauce and lemon juice and toss to combine.

6. Spoon the pilaf into a bowl, lay the fried fish pieces on top and scatter with coriander to serve.

Mary's Classic Tip:
* It's not essential to cook the peas if they are frozen; just stir them in and they will defrost and cook in the heat of the rice.

Cod & Crab Fishcakes

MAKES 6 fishcakes / CHILLING TIME: 10 minutes / COOK TIME: 35–40 minutes, plus cooling

Butter, for greasing and frying
350g (12oz) peeled potatoes, diced
300g (11oz) cod fillet, skinned
200g (7oz) fresh white crabmeat (see tip)
Juice of ½ lemon
2 tbsp snipped chives
1 rounded tsp Dijon mustard
25g (1oz) Parmesan cheese, grated
A few drops of Tabasco sauce
50g (2oz) panko breadcrumbs
1–2 tbsp oil
Salt and freshly ground black pepper

Prepare Ahead:
Can be made up to a day ahead and cooked to serve.

Freeze:
These freeze well uncooked.

Fishcakes are a favourite of mine. I keep them in the freezer individually wrapped and take them out when I know I am having a long busy day.

1. Preheat the oven to 200°C/180°C fan/Gas 6 and butter a sheet of foil for baking the cod.

2. Put the potatoes into a saucepan of cold salted water. Cover with a lid, bring to the boil and cook for about 15 minutes until soft. Drain well and then mash and set aside to cool.

3. Meanwhile, season the cod with salt and pepper and place on the buttered foil. Fold over the foil, sealing and scrunching up the edges to make a parcel, and place on a baking tray. Bake in the oven for 12–15 minutes until cooked through, then unwrap and leave to cool.

4. Place the cooled fish and mashed potato in a large bowl and add all of the remaining ingredients except the panko breadcrumbs and oil. Season well with salt and pepper and mix together. Shape into six even-sized balls and then flatten slightly into patties.

5. Sprinkle the panko breadcrumbs on a plate and coat each fishcake in the crumbs. Place in the fridge to chill for at least 10 minutes.

6. When ready to cook, heat a little oil and butter in a frying pan. When the butter has melted, fry the fishcakes on each side for 3–4 minutes until golden and crisp and heated through. You may need to do this in batches.

Mary's Classic Tip:
* If using fresh crabmeat, check before cooking that there are no little bones or shell in it. If you find it hard to get fresh crab, use tinned white crabmeat instead.

Smoked Haddock & Spinach Fish Pie

SERVES 6 / COOK TIME: 1 hour–1 hour 5 minutes

3 eggs
2 tbsp sunflower oil
2 medium leeks, cut into slices
    about 1.5cm (⅝in) thick
50g (2oz) butter
50g (2oz) plain flour
600ml (1 pint) hot milk
1 tbsp grainy mustard
750g (1¾lb) smoked
    haddock, skinned and
    sliced into large chunks
250g (9oz) baby spinach

For the topping
500g (1lb 2oz) peeled sweet
    potatoes, cut into even-
    sized cubes
500g (1lb 2oz) peeled
    potatoes, cut into even-
    sized cubes
A knob of butter
50g (2oz) mature Cheddar
    cheese, coarsely grated
Salt and freshly ground
    black pepper

You cannot beat a fish pie as a family favourite and for a modern classic, we have added sweet potato to the mash. This is a lovely recipe, hearty and filling with plenty of flavours.

1. You will need a 1.8–2.3-litre (3¼–4-pint) shallow ovenproof dish. Preheat the oven to 180°C/160°C fan/Gas 4.

2. First prepare the topping. Put the potatoes and sweet potatoes in a large saucepan of cold salted water and bring to the boil. Boil for about 15 minutes until tender, then drain well and return to the saucepan to mash. Add the butter and season with salt and pepper.

3. To boil the eggs, place in another saucepan of cold water, bring to the boil and cook for 6–7 minutes, then plunge into cold water to cool them quickly, changing the water again as it warms up. Peel the eggs as soon as they are cold, and slice into quarters.

4. Heat the sunflower oil in a large sauté pan or deep frying pan. Add the leeks and fry over a medium heat, stirring occasionally, for 10 minutes or until tender. Add the butter and stir until melted, then add the flour and stir to incorporate. Blend in the hot milk, stirring until you have a smooth, thickened sauce. Season well with salt and pepper and add the mustard.

5. Add the fish, mixing well to incorporate into the sauce, and allow to simmer for 1 minute. Spoon into the ovenproof dish and level the top.

6. Place the spinach in a large colander and pour over a kettleful of boiling water to wilt the leaves. Allow to cool, then squeeze out all of the liquid. Season with salt and pepper and arrange six mounds on top of the fish layer. Scatter over the egg quarters.

7. Spread the mashed potato on top of the fish and run a fork over the surface to make a nice pattern. Sprinkle with the grated cheese.

8. Bake in the oven for 30–35 minutes until golden on top and bubbling around the edges and the fish is cooked through (see tip).

Mary's Classic Tip:
* Pop a baking tray underneath the fish pie as it cooks to catch any sauce that bubbles over and that might otherwise burn on the base of the oven.

Poached Side of Salmon with Asparagus & Brown Shrimps

SERVES 8 / COOK TIME: 30 minutes, plus resting

Butter, for greasing
1 small bunch of dill
1kg (2lb 3oz) side of salmon fillet, skin on
50ml (2fl oz) white wine
Juice of 1 lemon
Salt and freshly ground black pepper

For the dressing
½ banana shallot, finely diced
2 tsp Dijon mustard
3 tbsp white wine vinegar
150ml (5fl oz) light olive oil
1 tsp caster sugar
1 bunch of dill, chopped

To garnish
20 asparagus tips, cut in half
100g (4oz) peeled cooked brown shrimps, patted dry
Pink radishes, sliced, and/or pink micro herbs

Prepare Ahead:
Assemble the dish up to 3 hours ahead. The salmon can be poached up to 8 hours ahead and the dressing made up to a week in advance.

This is a wonderful dish – so quick and simple to prepare, with great results. If you have a good fishmonger who will prepare the salmon well, nicely trimmed and pin-boned, there is very little to do except serving it up and impressing your guests.

1. Preheat the oven to 180°C/160°C fan/Gas 4. Lightly butter a large sheet of foil big enough to wrap the salmon, and place over a large roasting tin (see tip).

2. Place the dill in the centre of the foil. Season the buttered foil and place the salmon on top, skin side up. Pour over the wine and lemon juice. Bring the two long edges of the foil together and fold the edges, scrunching them into a parcel and sealing the edges like a Cornish pasty (see tip).

3. Place in the oven to poach for 25 minutes until the salmon is just cooked, the flesh pale pink and opaque. Leave to rest for 10 minutes, then remove the skin, pulling off in one piece if possible (see tip). Use a palette knife to scrape off grey fat.

4. Blanch the asparagus tips in a saucepan of boiling water for 3 minutes. Drain and refresh under cold water. Mix all of the dressing ingredients together in a jug and season.

5. Using two fish slices, transfer the salmon to a serving platter. Arrange the asparagus along the fish, scatter the shrimps over and spoon on some dressing. Garnish with radish and micro herbs and serve at room temperature with dressing in a jug.

Mary's Classic Tips:
* If you don't have a roasting tin large enough for the length of the piece of salmon, the grill pan makes a good alternative.
* Make sure you have a good seal around the edges of the foil parcel before baking to ensure no steam escapes.
* It is easier to remove the salmon skin while it is still warm; if the salmon cools down, the skin will stick firmly to the flesh.

Pan-Fried Squid Salad

SERVES 4–6 / PREP TIME: 15 minutes (to marinate) / COOK TIME: 1–3 minutes per batch of squid

500g (1¼lb) small squid,
   cleaned (see tips)
2 tbsp olive oil
Salt and freshly ground
   black pepper
½ fresh red chilli, deseeded
   and finely diced, to serve

For the dressing
1 tbsp Dijon mustard
Juice of 1 lemon
1 tbsp white wine vinegar
1 tbsp caster sugar
1 small garlic clove, crushed
12 tbsp (180ml/6fl oz)
   olive oil

For the salad
1 medium fennel bulb, core
   removed, thinly sliced
1 bunch of spring onions
   (about 6), sliced
200g (7oz) cherry tomatoes,
   halved
½ cucumber, halved
   lengthways, deseeded and
   sliced into crescent shapes
1 x 75g bag of mixed
   lettuce leaves

Prepare Ahead:
The squid and fennel can be
prepared up to 8 hours in
advance and left to marinate
in the oil/dressing.

This makes a lovely starter or light lunch. The crunchy fennel with its mild aniseed flavour and the mustardy dressing go well with the griddled squid.

1. Wash the squid thoroughly and pat dry, then slice each one in half lengthways and score one side of the flesh in a criss-cross pattern. Use the tip of a sharp knife to do this, taking care not to cut through the squid completely. Place in a bowl, along with any tentacles, and add the olive oil.

2. Mix all of the dressing ingredients together in a large bowl. Add the fennel and spring onions and leave to marinate for 15 minutes.

3. Heat a non-stick griddle pan or frying pan until hot. Season the squid with salt and pepper, then quickly fry on each side for about 1 minute until golden and cooked through. It will become opaque and start to curl. Cook the tentacles separately for 1–2 minutes.

4. Add the tomatoes, cucumber and lettuce to the fennel and spring onions in the bowl and toss together. Spoon the salad on to a plate and place the squid on top. Sprinkle over the chilli to serve.

Step-by-step images overleaf →

Mary's Classic Tips:
* At the supermarket fish counter, squid come ready-prepared and stuffed with the tentacles. Otherwise ask your fishmonger to do the hard work of cleaning and preparing them. If only large squid are available, cut them into 3–4 pieces, then cut each piece in half lengthways, as in step 1 above.
* You can otherwise use frozen (and defrosted) squid tubes; just remember to wash and pat them dry with kitchen paper before cooking.

Making the Pan-Fried Squid Salad:

POULTRY

·

GAME

Honey Chicken

SERVES 6 / MARINATE: A minimum of 30 minutes / COOK TIME: 35–40 minutes

6 chicken legs (about
  200g/7oz each), skin on
  (see tip)

For the marinade
6 tbsp tomato ketchup
2 tbsp tomato purée
2 tbsp grainy mustard
3 tbsp Worcestershire sauce
2 tbsp runny honey
1 garlic clove, crushed

Prepare Ahead:
Can be marinated up to
24 hours ahead. Serve cold
if preferred.

An old favourite of mine and one the family still love. Tender chicken that comes off the bone easily with a barbecue-style charred appearance and flavour. So easy – just put it in the oven and leave it to do its magic. If you would like smaller portions, use the same amount of thighs and drumsticks (six of each).

1. Using a sharp knife, make shallow slits in the top of the chicken legs (see tip).

2. Place all the ingredients for the marinade in a large bowl and stir until combined. Add the chicken legs and toss to coat, using your hands to cover them really well in the marinade. Cover the bowl and place in the fridge to marinate for a minimum of 30 minutes.

3. Meanwhile, preheat the oven to 220°C/200°C fan/Gas 7 and line a roasting tin with baking paper.

4. Place the marinated chicken legs in the lined tin, skin side up in a single layer, and spoon over the remaining marinade from the bowl. Roast in the oven for 35–40 minutes until sticky and golden and cooked through. Skim off any fat from the cooking juices and pour the juices into a jug.

5. Serve hot with the juices poured over, and with a green vegetable and sauté potatoes or mash (see page 177) on the side.

Mary's Classic Tips:
* Remove the skin from the chicken legs, if you prefer.
* Don't forget to wash your hands after handling raw poultry.

Roast Chicken Thighs with Sweet Potato & Cauliflower

SERVES 4–8 / MARINATE: A minimum of 30 minutes / COOK TIME: 30–40 minutes

8 chicken thighs on the bone
(about 150g/5oz each),
skin on

For the marinade
2 tbsp olive oil
1 garlic clove, crushed
1 tsp chopped thyme leaves
Juice and finely grated zest
of ½ lemon
½ fresh red chilli, deseeded
and finely chopped

For the vegetables
400g (14oz) sweet potatoes,
peeled and cut into 1.5cm
(⅝in) cubes
200g (7oz) potatoes, peeled
and cut into 1.5cm
(⅝in) cubes
1 small cauliflower, cut into
tiny florets (similar in size
to the potato cubes)
1 onion, sliced
3 celery sticks, sliced
2 tbsp olive oil
4 bay leaves
6 rashers of smoked streaky
bacon, cut into small pieces
Salt and freshly ground
black pepper

The chicken skin is crisp and full of flavour, the vegetable combination works well and the bacon really adds to the overall flavour. The cauliflower also becomes nicely charred while the potatoes soften. This recipe can be put in the oven and forgotten about – no need to baste or turn as the chicken bastes the vegetables and the juices give a thin but tasty sauce.

1. Preheat the oven to 220°C/200°C fan/Gas 7.

2. Place the marinade ingredients in a bowl or large freezer bag and mix to combine. Add the chicken thighs and coat in the mixture, then transfer to the fridge to marinate for a minimum of 30 minutes.

3. Put all the vegetables into a large shallow roasting tin, add the oil and season with salt and pepper. Toss together so the vegetables are coated in the oil. Arrange the marinated chicken thighs on top, skin side up, then scatter over the bay leaves and bacon pieces.

4. Roast in the oven for 30–40 minutes until the chicken is tender and golden brown (see tip). Remove the bay leaves and serve immediately.

Prepare Ahead:
The chicken can be left to marinate in the fridge up to a day ahead.

Mary's Classic Tips:
* Take care not to overcook. It's best to rest the chicken thighs after they come out of the oven to keep them moist.

Herb Roast Poussin with Aioli

SERVES 6 / MARINATE: A minimum of 3 hours / COOK TIME: 30–40 minutes, plus resting

3 poussins (about 500g/
  1lb 2oz each)
2 tbsp chopped
  rosemary leaves
2 tbsp olive oil
2 tbsp runny honey
2 garlic cloves, crushed
Salt and freshly ground
  black pepper

For the aioli
6 tbsp full-fat mayonnaise
  (see tip)
4 tbsp full-fat crème fraîche
4 tbsp chopped parsley
1 small garlic clove
Juice of ½ lemon
1 tsp caster sugar
Salt and freshly ground
  black pepper

Prepare Ahead:
Marinade the poussins up to
2 days ahead and keep stored
in the fridge. The aioli can be
made up to 3 days ahead –
the flavours will become
more intense.

Freeze:
The poussins can be frozen,
uncooked, in the marinade.

Classic flavours and classic technique, one of my favourite dishes. Marinating the poussins in the bag is a great tip. It's a good way to massage all the flavours into the birds without handling raw poultry again. The poussins also sit nicely in the bag in the fridge, covered and taking up less space than a plate.

1. First spatchcock each poussin – or ask your butcher to do this. Cut either side of the backbone with a large kitchen knife, poultry shears or even a pair of sturdy kitchen scissors. Cut the backbone free and discard. Turn the poussin breast side up, place the palm of your hand on the breastbone and press until flat. (You will hear an audible crunch.)

2. Measure the rosemary leaves, olive oil and honey into a freezer bag, add the garlic and the poussins and massage the flavourings into the birds, making sure each is well coated. Leave to marinate in the fridge between 3 and 24 hours.

3. When you are ready to cook the poussins, preheat the oven to 200°C/180°C fan/Gas 6.

4. Sit the marinated poussins in a shallow roasting tin, breast side up, and season. Tip any marinade over the birds and roast for 30–40 minutes until golden brown and the juices run clear. Leave to rest for about 10 minutes (see tip).

5. Mix all the aioli ingredients together in a bowl and season.

6. Carve each bird in half and serve with the aioli and some sauté potatoes and greens beans.

Mary's Classic Tips:
∗ To measure out creamy mayo and crème fraîche easily, first wet the measuring spoon in cold water, before spooning out the required amount. The spoonfuls will slide off easily, leaving a clean spoon that's ready to measure out the rest.
∗ The cooking juices from the poussins make a fabulous gravy. If you don't want gravy this time, don't waste it. Make a quick gravy from the juices and freeze it to use on another occasion.

Chicken Supreme with Mushrooms & Bacon

SERVES 6 / COOK TIME: 40 minutes

2–3 tbsp olive oil

6 chicken breasts, skin on

4 banana shallots, thinly sliced

200g (7oz) rashers of smoked
   streaky bacon, cut into
   small pieces

2 garlic cloves, crushed

600ml (1 pint) chicken stock

150ml (5fl oz) sherry

25g (1oz) plain flour

1 tsp white wine vinegar

100ml (3½fl oz) double cream

A large knob of butter

450g (1lb) mixed chestnut
   and wild mushrooms,
   thickly sliced

Salt and freshly ground
   black pepper

A dish full of flavour and perfect for making ahead and feeding to a crowd.

1. Preheat the oven to 200°C/160°C fan/Gas 6.

2. Heat 2 tablespoons of the oil in a large flameproof and ovenproof casserole dish with a lid (see tip). Season the chicken breasts with salt and pepper, then place them, skin side down, in the dish and brown over a high heat for about 4–5 minutes until golden and crisp (see tip). Transfer to a plate lined with kitchen paper to soak up any excess oil.

3. Add a dash more oil to the dish, if needed, then tip in the shallots and bacon and fry over a high heat for about 5 minutes, stirring, until the bacon is crisp (see tip). Add the garlic and stir in.

4. Boil the stock in a small saucepan until it has reduced by about half.

5. Add the sherry to the casserole dish and boil to deglaze the base of the pan. Measure the flour into a bowl, mix in 6 tablespoons of cold water and stir until smooth. Pour in a little of the hot stock and stir it into the flour mixture. Add the remaining stock and the flour mixture to the casserole dish and stir in. Add the vinegar and cream, season with salt and pepper and bring to the boil.

6. Return the chicken to the pan, then bring back up to the boil, cover with the lid and transfer to the oven to cook for 12–15 minutes or until the chicken is cooked (see tip).

Prepare Ahead:
Can be made up to a day
ahead and reheated.

....

Freeze:
The cooked dish freezes well
without the mushrooms. Add
the freshly cooked mushrooms
to the dish once it's reheated
and ready to serve.

7. When ready to serve, melt the butter in a large frying pan
    and fry the mushrooms over a high heat for 4–5 minutes
    until just golden. Season with salt and pepper, then spoon
    half the cooked mushrooms into the casserole dish and
    mix well.

8. Divide the chicken among the plates and sprinkle with the
    remaining golden mushrooms to serve.

Mary's Classic Tips:
* If you haven't a large casserole, use a large non-stick frying
  pan with a lid.
* Take the time to get a really good golden colour on the
  chicken skin in the first stage of cooking – the golden breast
  looks really attractive in the sauce, and this adds flavour to the
  dish too. It also ensures the chicken is partially cooked by the
  time it goes into the oven, so that it needs only a relatively
  short time to finish cooking.
* Keep the heat nice and high when the shallots and bacon are
  frying, so the bacon crisps and browns. If the heat is too low,
  the bacon can 'stew' in the juices, rather than crisping nicely.
* Cut into the thickest part of the largest chicken breast to
  check that the meat is cooked through, with no pink showing.
  If it's not quite cooked, pop it back in the oven for another
  few minutes.

Malayan Chicken Curry

SERVES 4–6 / COOK TIME: 25–30 minutes

2–3 tbsp sunflower oil

4 large skinless and boneless
   chicken breasts, sliced into
   3cm (1¼in) pieces

2 large onions, sliced

2cm (¾in) knob of fresh root
   ginger, peeled and grated
   (see tip)

2 large garlic cloves, crushed

1 tbsp medium curry powder

½ tsp turmeric powder

¼ tsp ground cloves

200ml (7fl oz) chicken stock

1 tbsp mango chutney, plus
   extra to serve

200ml (7fl oz) double cream

4 dried curry leaves

Salt and freshly ground
   black pepper

A few sprigs of coriander,
   to serve

Prepare Ahead:
Can be made up to a day
ahead and reheated.

Freeze:
Freezes well.

Classic, rich and deep in flavour. My husband lived in Malaysia, Malaya as it was then, for a time in his youth so he loves a homemade curry. He raved about this one – lovely, authentic-tasting flavours.

1. Heat 2 tablespoons of the oil in a large deep frying pan. Season the chicken with salt and pepper and fry in two batches over a high heat for 3–4 minutes until golden and sealed. Remove from the pan and set aside.

2. Add the remaining oil if needed, tip in the onions and fry over a medium heat for 10 minutes until soft. Add the ginger, garlic and spices and fry for between 30 seconds and 1 minute. Pour in the stock, add the mango chutney and bring to the boil. Boil for a couple of minutes to reduce the liquid slightly, then add the cream and curry leaves and season with salt and pepper.

3. Bring back up to the boil, then add the chicken, cover with a lid and gently simmer for 5 minutes until the chicken is cooked through.

4. Remove the curry leaves, decorate with the coriander and serve with rice and extra mango chutney.

Mary's Classic Tip:
* Don't waste any leftover root ginger. A knob of ginger freezes really well and can be grated straight from the freezer, so you always have some to hand.

Chicken Noodle Soup

SERVES 4–6 / COOK TIME: 40–45 minutes

1.5 litres (2½ pints) chicken stock (see tip)
4 skinless and boneless chicken thighs
1 tbsp olive oil
1 onion, chopped
2 celery sticks, sliced
100g (4oz) button mushrooms, sliced
½ fresh red chilli, deseeded and diced
1 tbsp soy sauce
1 tbsp sweet chilli sauce
100g (4oz) fine egg noodles (see tip)
Salt and freshly ground black pepper
2–3 tbsp chopped coriander, to garnish

Prepare Ahead:
The soup can be made up to 4 hours ahead and reheated. The chicken can be cooked up to a day in advance, then cooled completely and stored in the fridge; be sure to heat the chicken through thoroughly before serving.

A meal in itself – a good, healthy main course – this makes an authentic chicken noodle soup without a hint of MSG or dried seasonings! A good way to use up shredded leftover roast chicken – use around 300g (11oz).

1. Measure the stock into a large saucepan, add the chicken thighs and bring to the boil. Allow to boil for a few minutes, then reduce the heat, cover with a lid and simmer for 20 minutes until tender. Remove the chicken and set aside to cool slightly.

2. Heat the oil in wide-based saucepan, add the onion and celery and fry over a high heat for 3–4 minutes. Add the mushrooms and diced chilli and fry for a minute. Pour in the stock and bring to boil, then reduce the heat and season with salt and pepper. Add the soy sauce and chilli sauce, cover with a lid and simmer for about 5 minutes.

3. Meanwhile, shred the chicken, removing any skin – using two forks to pull the meat apart.

4. Return the soup to the boil, add the chicken and noodles and cook according to the packet instructions (about 5 minutes) until the noodles are tender.

5. Spoon into bowls and scatter with coriander to serve.

Mary's Classic Tips:
* Use the best stock possible for this dish: the better the flavour, the tastier the soup.
* Break the dried noodles in half before cooking them, if you prefer, to make it easier to serve and eat them.

Chicken with Tomato, Mozzarella & Basil

SERVES 4 / COOK TIME: 15 minutes

3 tbsp olive oil

1 onion, finely chopped

1 garlic clove, crushed

1 beef tomato,
   roughly chopped

400g (14oz) plum tomatoes,
   roughly chopped

200g (7oz) cherry tomatoes,
   halved

1 large bunch of basil,
   chopped

50g (2oz) pine nuts, toasted
   (see tip on page 82)

250g (9oz) mozzarella, torn
   into large pieces (see tip)

2 tbsp balsamic vinegar

2 skinless and boneless
   chicken breasts

Sea salt flakes, to serve

For the pesto dressing

1 large bunch of basil

1 garlic clove, crushed

1 tsp white wine vinegar

6 tbsp olive oil

50g (2oz) pine nuts, toasted
   (see tip on page 82)

1 tsp sugar

25g (1oz) Parmesan cheese,
   roughly grated

Salt and freshly ground
   black pepper

Prepare Ahead:
Can be assembled up to
2 hours ahead.

Chicken with an Italian twist. Choose good-quality tomatoes that are full of flavour. It's worth paying for the best for this recipe. If you buy them on the vine, the flavour is usually better.

1. To make the pesto dressing, place all the dressing ingredients in a food processor and whizz until nearly smooth. Scrape down the sides of the processor with a rubber spatula as needed and season to taste with salt and pepper.

2. Heat 1 tablespoon of the olive oil in a frying pan, add the onion and garlic and fry over a medium heat for about 4 minutes until nearly soft. Spoon into a large bowl. Add all the tomatoes, along with the basil, pine nuts, mozzarella and balsamic vinegar, then season and toss together.

3. Heat the remaining oil in the frying pan, add the chicken and pan-fry for 3–5 minutes on each side or until lightly golden and cooked through. Set aside to rest for 2 minutes.

4. Spoon the tomato and mozzarella salad on to a serving platter, then slice the chicken and arrange on top. Drizzle over the pesto dressing, season with sea salt flakes and serve with crunchy bread (see tip).

Mary's Classic Tips:
* Use a good-quality mozzarella that will tear nicely yet still keep its shape.
* If you have any salad left over, tear up some stale bread and toss it in with the tomatoes and their juices for an Italian 'panzanella'-style salad.

Chicken, Avocado & Bacon Salad

SERVES 8–10 / MARINATE: A minimum of 2 hours / COOK TIME: 4–5 minutes (for the bacon)

1 cooked chicken (about
   600g/1lb 5oz)
6 rashers of smoked
   streaky bacon
2 Little Gem lettuces
50g (2oz) rocket
2 small avocados
25g (1oz) pumpkin seeds,
   toasted (see tip)

For the dressing
300ml (10fl oz)
   natural yoghurt
Juice of ½ lemon
1 tbsp chopped
   tarragon leaves
2 small spring onions,
   finely sliced
1 tbsp Dijon mustard
1 tsp caster sugar
2 tsp white wine vinegar
Salt and freshly ground
   black pepper

Prepare Ahead:
The chicken can be
marinated up to 24 hours
ahead. Assemble the dish,
minus the avocado, up to
2 hours in advance, then
peel and slice the avocado
and add to the platter just
before serving to prevent
it discolouring.

An impressive and attractive salad platter: easy to assemble with other salads and take to the table for a light lunch or supper with friends. Full of flavour and texture with peppery rocket, a creamy dressing with a subtle tarragon flavour, crunchy bacon and on-trend ingredients avocado and roasted pumpkin seeds.

1. Remove the skin from the chicken, then carve the meat and slice it into pieces.

2. Place all of the ingredients for the dressing in a bowl and season well with salt and pepper. Add the chicken pieces and stir to coat in the mixture. Cover the bowl and leave to marinate in the fridge for 2 hours or overnight.

3. Shortly before you are ready to serve, cook the bacon under the grill or in a dry pan for 4–5 minutes until crisp and golden. Set aside to drain on a piece of kitchen paper. Once cold, snip into little pieces.

4. On a large platter, place two to three lettuce leaves next to each other and slightly overlapping to make a cup shape. Top with some rocket leaves. Repeat with the remaining lettuce and rocket, so that you have 8–10 lettuce cups arranged in a circle to look like a wreath.

5. Spoon the chicken salad on top. Peel and slice the avocado and place three slices on top of each of the chicken-filled lettuce cups. Sprinkle with the bacon pieces and toasted pumpkin seeds. Season with a little salt and pepper and serve.

Mary's Classic Tip:
* To toast pumpkin or other seeds, place in a dry pan and toss over a medium heat for 1–2 minutes or until golden brown. Keep an eye on them as they burn easily.

Chicken, Halloumi & Watercress Salad

SERVES 6 / MARINATE: A minimum of 15 minutes / COOK TIME: 10 minutes

2 skinless and boneless
   chicken breasts, cut into
   thin strips
1 tbsp chopped marjoram
Finely grated zest of 1 lemon
2 tbsp olive oil
100g (4oz) watercress
½ cucumber
½ red onion, sliced
1 x 180g jar of roasted red
   peppers, sliced into strips
250g (9oz) halloumi cheese,
   cut into 1.5cm (⅝in) slices
Salt and freshly ground
   black pepper

For the dressing
150ml (5fl oz)
   natural yoghurt
1 tsp white wine vinegar
Juice of 1 lemon
½ garlic clove, crushed
1 tsp ground cumin
1 tsp sugar

Prepare Ahead:
Marinate the chicken up to a
day ahead, keeping it stored
in the fridge. The dressing
can be made up to a day in
advance and kept in the
fridge too.

I will admit it took me a little while to like halloumi, but I think that was because any I had tasted was rubbery when cooked! It must be cooked on high for short time – now it's lovely! This would make a nice vegetarian meal if you left out the chicken.

1. Place the chicken in a dish and add the marjoram, lemon zest and olive oil. Season with salt and pepper, then toss together and leave to marinate for a minimum of 15 minutes.

2. Place the watercress in a large bowl or platter. Peel the cucumber and cut in half lengthways, then remove the seeds and slice the cucumber into thin crescents. Scatter these over the watercress, along with the onion and roasted peppers, and season with salt and pepper.

3. Measure all the dressing ingredients into a bowl and mix together, seasoning to taste with salt and pepper.

4. Heat a griddle pan or frying pan until piping hot. Add the marinated chicken and fry for about 3 minutes on one side, then turn over and fry for 2 minutes on the other side until cooked through and golden. Set aside and keep warm.

5. Wipe the hot pan carefully with kitchen paper and return to the heat. When the pan is very hot, fry the halloumi slices for a minute on each side until chargrilled (see tip).

6. Arrange the hot chicken and halloumi over the salad and pour over the dressing to serve.

Mary's Classic Tip:
* When frying the halloumi, don't be tempted to move it before it is cooked as it will stick to the pan and tear. Leave it for at least a minute and lift a corner to see if it is ready to turn. If it lifts easily, it's ready; if it resists, then leave it for a little longer.

Warm Chicken Liver Salad with a Hint of Pomegranate

SERVES 6 / COOK TIME: 25 minutes

75g (3oz) quinoa

100g (4oz) rashers of smoked streaky bacon, chopped into pieces

1 x 70g bag of rocket leaves

2 heads of red chicory, quartered lengthways and core removed

125g (4½oz) pomegranate seeds (seeds of 1 large pomegranate)

50g (2oz) pine nuts, toasted (see tip on page 82)

A knob of butter

400g (14oz) fresh chicken livers, trimmed

Salt and freshly ground black pepper

For the dressing

1 tbsp grainy mustard

1 heaped tsp muscovado sugar

3 tbsp pomegranate syrup (see tip)

8 tbsp olive oil

A modern way to serve liver and bacon, soft and tender with on-trend quinoa and pomegranate. I served this to friends who all agreed it was nothing like the liver they remembered from their childhoods!

1. Cook the quinoa in boiling water according to the packet instructions, then drain and run under cold water.

2. Dry-fry the bacon in a large frying pan over a high heat for 3–4 minutes until crispy, then set aside.

3. Scatter the rocket over a platter and arrange the chicory quarters on top. Sprinkle with the pomegranate seeds, cooked quinoa and toasted pine nuts.

4. Whisk all the dressing ingredients together.

5. Melt the butter in the frying pan, season the chicken livers with salt and pepper and fry over a high heat on each side for about 2 minutes until golden on the outside and just pink in the middle.

6. Arrange the livers over the salad, scatter the crispy bacon pieces on top and pour over the dressing to serve

Prepare Ahead:
The basic salad can be assembled up to 2 hours ahead, the liver, bacon and dressing added to serve.

Mary's Classic Tip:
* Pomegranate syrup is also known as pomegranate molasses. If you can't find it, you could use a sweet white balsamic vinegar instead.

Chicken Normande

SERVES 6 / COOK TIME: 1 hour

6 chicken thighs on the bone
(see tip), skin removed
2 tbsp oil
30g (1oz) butter
400g (14oz) banana shallots,
sliced
5 celery sticks, sliced
2 garlic cloves, crushed
150ml (5fl oz) Calvados
or brandy
30g (1oz) plain flour
200ml (7fl oz) chicken stock
3 eating apples, peeled, cored
and sliced into wedges
1–2cm (½–¾in) thick
1 tsp muscovado sugar
200ml (7fl oz) full-fat
crème fraîche
Salt and freshly ground
black pepper
1 tbsp chopped parsley,
to serve

Prepare Ahead:
Can be made up to a day
ahead. Add the crème fraîche
and fry the apples to serve.

Freeze:
Freezes well without the
crème fraîche and apples.

A classic – 'Normande' implying apple. A mild and creamy apple-flavoured dish.

1. Preheat the oven to 160°C/140°C fan/Gas 3.

2. Season the chicken thighs with salt and pepper. Heat the oil and half the butter in a deep ovenproof saucepan or flameproof and ovenproof casserole dish. When the butter has melted, brown the chicken on all sides over a high heat for 4–5 minutes until golden. You may need to do this in batches. Remove from the pan and set aside.

3. Add the shallots and celery to the pan and fry over a high heat for 4–5 minutes. Add the garlic and fry for a further 1–2 minutes. Pour in the Calvados or brandy and boil for a few seconds.

4. Measure the flour into a bowl, add 3 tablespoons of the stock and blend until smooth. Gradually blend in the rest of the stock, then add to the pan, bring to the boil, stirring, and cook until smooth and thickened. Return the chicken pieces to the pan and season with salt and pepper. Cover with a lid, bring back up to the boil and transfer to the oven to cook for about 40 minutes or until tender.

5. When ready to serve, fry the apple in the remaining butter, sprinkle over the sugar and fry over a high heat for 4–5 minutes until golden.

6. Stir the crème fraîche into the pan with the chicken, check the seasoning and serve with a sprinkling of parsley and a spoonful of golden apple slices on the top.

Step-by-step images overleaf →

Mary's Classic Tip:
* You can substitute with six skinless chicken breasts,
if you prefer.

Making the Chicken Normande:

Slow-Roast Duck with Port & Cherry Sauce

SERVES 4–6 / COOK TIME: 3½ hours, plus resting

1.8–2kg (4lb–4¼lb) whole
    duck without giblets (see tip)
Sunflower oil (for rubbing
    into the duck's skin)
Salt and freshly ground
    black pepper

For the cherry sauce
3 shallots, chopped
150ml (5fl oz) port
150ml (5fl oz) red wine
300ml (10fl oz) chicken stock
2 tbsp redcurrant jelly
1½ tsp balsamic vinegar
200g (7oz) frozen pitted
    cherries (defrosted)
2½ tbsp cornflour

Prepare Ahead:
The sauce can be made up to
a day ahead and reheated.
The duck can be roasted
8 hours ahead if serving cold.

Duck à l'orange and duck with cherry sauce – such classic recipes. Originally the cherries would have to be fresh so the time of year was restricted; now use fresh or the frozen ones are excellent too. A cross between Chinese crispy duck and standard roast duck – plenty of crisp skin with fall-apart moist and tender meat. The sauce has a delicious sweet-and-savoury note to it, and is beautifully glossy.

1. Preheat the oven to 220°C/200°C fan/Gas 7.

2. Sit the duck, breast side up, on a trivet in a roasting tin and dry the skin with kitchen paper – the drier it is the crisper the cooked skin will be. Rub the skin with oil and season with salt.

3. Roast in the oven for about 30 minutes or until golden. Reduce the oven temperature to 160°C/140°C fan/Gas 3 and slow-roast for 2½ hours, basting from time to time. The wings of the duck should be tender, and the legs should come away easily from the body of the bird.

4. Drain the fat from the bottom of the tin, reserving about 1 tablespoon for cooking the sauce (see tip). Increase the oven temperature to 220°C/200°C fan/Gas 7 and return the tin to the oven for 20–30 minutes or until the skin of the duck is golden and crisp. Remove from the oven to rest for 15 minutes before carving.

5. Meanwhile, make the sauce. Heat the reserved duck fat in a medium saucepan and fry the shallots over a medium-high heat for 4–5 minutes until lightly golden but not burnt. Pour in the port, wine and stock, then raise the heat and allow to bubble for 5–10 minutes until reduced by a third.

Continued overleaf →

6. Add the jelly and vinegar, then strain the sauce and discard the shallots. Mix the cornflour with 3 tablespoons of water in a small bowl until smooth. Add a little of the hot sauce to the bowl and then add the mixture to the rest of the sauce in the pan. Add the cherries and carefully bring to the boil, stirring. Season with salt and pepper and boil until the sauce is glossy and thick enough to coat the back of a spoon.

7. Carve the duck – it will be very tender and cooked through, not pink like a duck breast – and serve with the cherry sauce

Mary's Classic Tips:

* If your duck comes with the giblets, save them to make a flavoursome stock with the duck bones. It freezes well and can be used in place of the chicken stock used here. Or use for the game stock suggested for the roast pheasant on page 94.

* Keep the duck fat – it's great for flavoursome roast potatoes.

Pot-Roast Pheasant with Calvados

SERVES 6–8 / COOK TIME: 1 hour 5 minutes

1 tbsp oil

30g (1oz) butter

2 oven-ready pheasants
(around 900g/2lb in total)

2 onions, sliced

30g (1oz) plain flour

150ml (5fl oz) Calvados or
brandy

450ml (15fl oz) game or
chicken stock

2 sprigs of thyme

4 rashers of smoked streaky
bacon, sliced into pieces

400g (14oz) button
mushrooms

2 eating apples

3 tbsp double cream

Salt and freshly ground
black pepper

This uses all the bird, but if you are not so keen on the drumsticks use for stock after cooking. Frying then adding the apple at the end adds colour and keeps its texture, and the flavour complements the pheasant well.

1. You will need a 4-litre (7-pint) deep flameproof and ovenproof casserole dish with a lid. Preheat the oven to 180°C/160°C fan/Gas 4.

2. Heat the oil and half the butter in the casserole dish and, when the butter has melted, brown the pheasants on all sides over a high heat for 5–8 minutes until golden. Brown the pheasants one at a time, if it is easier, then remove from the pan and set aside.

3. Add the onions and fry over a medium heat for 2–3 minutes, then cover with the lid and cook on a low heat for 5 minutes until softened.

4. Measure the flour and Calvados or brandy into a jug or bowl and whisk until smooth. Whisk in the stock a little at a time. Add the liquid to the casserole dish and stir until thickened and smooth. Return the pheasants to the dish, then add thyme and bring to the boil. Season with salt and pepper, cover and transfer to the oven to cook for about 40 minutes.

5. Meanwhile, dry-fry the bacon in a non-stick frying pan over a high heat for 4–5 minutes until crisp, stirring to break up the pieces and make sure they brown evenly (see tip). Remove with a slotted spoon. Melt the remaining butter in the pan, add the mushrooms and fry over a medium heat for 3–4 minutes until golden, then set aside with the bacon.

Can be made up to a day
ahead and reheated.

....

Freezes well.

6. Peel and core the apples and slice each into 12 wedges, then add to the pan and fry until golden but not too soft. Add the bacon, mushrooms and apples to the casserole dish and cook in the oven for a further 10 minutes.

7. Remove the dish from the oven, take out the birds and cut off the legs, jointing these into two, to give a thigh and drumstick (see tip). Remove the breasts from each carcass and slice into thick slices. Arrange the meat on a large warmed platter, cover with foil and leave to rest.

8. Meanwhile, add the cream to the pan with any juices and bring to the boil. Remove from the heat and take out the thyme sprigs, then check the seasoning and pour the sauce with the apples and mushrooms over the meat on the platter.

9. Serve piping hot with mash (see page 177) and a green vegetable, such as tender-stem broccoli.

Mary's Classic Tips:
* You can fry the bacon rashers whole, if you prefer, and snip into pieces with scissors once cooked.
* If the legs are still slightly pink, pop them back in the oven on a baking tray to cook for slightly longer, if preferred, although it is acceptable to eat pheasant slightly pink.

Royal Guineafowl Casserole

SERVES 6 / COOK TIME: 1 hour 10 minutes

2 guineafowl
2 tbsp oil
30g (1oz) butter
675g (1½lb) shallots (see tip),
   thickly sliced
2 garlic cloves, crushed
1 tsp muscovado sugar
2 tsp balsamic vinegar
30g (1oz) plain flour
450ml (15fl oz) white wine
300ml (10fl oz) double cream
2 tbsp chopped tarragon
2 tbsp chopped parsley
500g (1lb 2oz) chestnut
   mushrooms, halved
Salt and freshly ground
   black pepper

With its herb mushroom sauce, this casserole would grace any royal feast.

1. Preheat the oven to 160°C/140°C Fan/Gas 3.

2. Joint the guineafowl and remove the legs (the whole leg, with the thigh and drumstick in one piece) and breast from the bone, so you have four legs and four breasts (see tip). Season with salt and pepper.

3. Heat 1 tablespoon of the oil and half the butter in a deep ovenproof frying pan or flameproof and ovenproof casserole dish. When the butter has melted, brown the joints over a high heat until golden all over – you may need to do this in batches. Remove from the pan and set aside.

4. Add the remaining oil if needed, tip in the shallots and fry over a high heat, stirring frequently, for 4–5 minutes. Add the garlic, sugar and vinegar and fry for another 2–3 minutes until the shallots start to become golden.

5. Measure the flour into a large bowl and gradually whisk in the wine, a little at a time, until you have a smooth paste, then add the rest to make a cloudy liquid. Pour into the pan and stir over the heat until thickened and smooth. Season with salt and pepper, then return the leg joints to the pan.

Continued overleaf →

6. Bring to the boil, cover with a lid and transfer to the oven to cook for about 20 minutes. Add the breasts, mixing them into the sauce, and return to the oven to cook for a further 15 minutes or until tender.

7. Stir in the cream and add the tarragon and parsley, then check the seasoning.

8. In a large frying pan, fry the mushrooms over a medium-high heat in the rest of the butter for 3–4 minutes until golden, and add to the casserole. Serve piping hot with vegetables and potatoes of your choice.

Prepare Ahead:
The casserole can be made up to a day ahead, adding the fresh herbs and mushrooms to serve.

Freeze:
Freezes well; omit the herbs and mushrooms and add to serve.

Mary's Classic Tips:
* For a speedy way to peel a large quantity of shallots, leave them in a bowl of boiling water for 4–5 minutes, then remove and, when cool enough to handle, you'll find it easy to slip off the skins.
* If you're unsure about jointing the guineafowl, ask your butcher to do it for you.

Roast Partridge with Plum Sauce

SERVES 4 / COOK TIME: 30 minutes, plus resting

2 oven-ready partridge
2 bay leaves
2 sprigs of rosemary
Oil, for rubbing into
   the skin
2 rashers of streaky bacon
2 tsp maple syrup
Salt and freshly ground
   black pepper

For the plum sauce
1 tbsp oil
1 onion, finely chopped
250g (9oz) stoned plums,
   quartered
1 garlic clove, crushed
1 tsp coarsely grated fresh
   root ginger
1 tsp good balsamic vinegar
1 tbsp light muscovado sugar
1 tbsp soy sauce
200ml (7fl oz) chicken
   or game stock
A dash of gravy browning

Prepare Ahead:
The sauce can be made up
to a day ahead.

A really nice change for a special occasion, this classic from years gone by is lovely served with a fruit or slightly sweet sauce. Game meat can be dry so the gingery plum sauce keeps it nice and moist.

1. Preheat the oven to 220°C/200°C fan/Gas 7.

2. Sit the partridge in a small roasting tin. Push a bay leaf and a rosemary sprig into the cavity of each bird. Rub some oil over the breasts and legs, and season with salt and pepper. Lay the bacon across the breasts, cutting the rashers in half if they are too long, and drizzle over the maple syrup.

3. Roast in the oven for about 30 minutes until golden all over and cooked through – check the juices run clear by inserting a sharp knife into the thickest part of the thigh. Cover with foil and leave to rest for 10–15 minutes.

4. While the partridge are roasting, make the sauce. Heat the oil in a large saucepan, add the onion and fry over a high heat for 2–3 minutes. Add the plums, garlic and ginger and fry for a further minute. Add the vinegar, sugar and soy sauce and cook for another 2–3 minutes until the onions have darkened in colour.

5. Pour in the stock and bring to the boil. Lower the heat, cover with a lid and simmer for about 10 minutes until the onion and plums are soft. Blend until smooth, either with a hand blender or in a free-standing blender or food processer (see tip). Add a dash of gravy browning for colour and check the seasoning.

6. Carve the legs from the birds and slice the breasts, then serve with the hot sauce.

Mary's Classic Tip:
* If you're using a hand blender to blend the plum sauce, you may need to transfer it first to a jug or high-sided bowl, to make sure the sauce is a deep enough to blend and is contained well.

PORK

·

LAMB

·

BEEF

Ginger Gammon with Mustard Sauce

SERVES 6–8 / COOK TIME: 3½ hours

2.7kg (6lb) boneless
  unsmoked gammon
  (see tip)
600ml (1 pint) ginger beer
4 tbsp ginger syrup (from
  the jar)
4 stem ginger bulbs,
  finely chopped

For the mustard sauce
200ml (7fl oz) full-fat
  crème fraîche
6 tbsp full-fat mayonnaise
2 tbsp Dijon mustard
2 tbsp grainy mustard
A pinch of caster sugar
Salt and freshly ground
  black pepper

Prepare Ahead:
Once cooked, the gammon
keeps well in the fridge for
2–3 days. The sauce can be
made in advance and stored
in the fridge for 1–2 days.

Mary's Classic Tip:
* You may want to soak the
  gammon and refresh the
  water before cooking to
  help remove any excess salt.

Perfect to feed numbers and can be served hot or cold. Ham is cooked and gammon is raw and cured in the same way as bacon. The long, slow cooking (in the oven or on the hob) means that the gammon pulls apart and has a melt-in-the-mouth texture. The ginger and syrup give a lovely flavour, while the mustard sauce is punchy. Ideally serve hot and have any leftovers cold the next day.

1. Preheat the oven to 160°C/140°C fan/Gas 3.

2. Put the ham in an ovenproof saucepan large enough for it to fit snugly. Pour in the ginger beer and 1.1 litres (2 pints) of water or just enough to cover the gammon. Cover with a lid, bring to the boil and allow to boil for a few minutes, using a slotted spoon to skim off any scum that forms.

3. Transfer to the oven to cook for about 3 hours or until cooked through. Alternatively, simmer over a low heat on the hob for about 3 hours. Check the gammon occasionally, to make sure enough liquid remains in the pan.

4. Increase the oven temperature to 220°C/200°C fan/Gas 7 and line a roasting tin with foil.

5. Remove the gammon from the cooking liquid and, using a sharp knife, slice off the skin so that only a very thin layer of fat is left. Sit the gammon, fat side up, in the lined tin. Score the fat, then drizzle over the ginger syrup and scatter over the chopped ginger, pressing lightly so the ginger studs the top of the fat.

6. Bake in the oven for about 25 minutes or until golden and glazed on top, basting halfway through with any juices. Watch out as the sugar syrup easily burns on to the tin, although the foil does help to protect it.

7. To make the mustard sauce, mix all the ingredients together and season with salt and pepper.

8. Slice the gammon into thin slices and serve, hot or cold, with the sauce

One-Tray Sausage Supper

SERVES 4–6 / COOK TIME: 50 minutes

500g (1lb 2oz) Chantenay
  carrots (scrubbed or
  peeled, as needed)
1kg (2lb 3oz) large potatoes,
  peeled and diced into
  2.5cm (1in) cubes
2 tbsp oil
50g (2oz) butter
500g (1lb 2oz) raw beetroot,
  peeled and diced into 1.5cm
  (⅝in) cubes (see tip)
1 large onion, sliced
2 garlic cloves, crushed
12 good butcher's
  pork sausages
50g (2oz) Parmesan
  cheese, grated
Salt and freshly ground
  black pepper

**An all-in-one dish with root veg and your favourite sausages.
Perfect with the big fat butcher's sausages.**

1. Preheat the oven to 220°C/200°C Fan/Gas 7.

2. Bring a saucepan of salted water to the boil. Add the carrots
    and potatoes and boil for about 4 minutes, then drain well.

3. Meanwhile, place the oil and butter in a large roasting tin
    and heat in the oven. Add the drained vegetables to the tin,
    with the beetroot, onion and garlic, season with salt and
    pepper and toss in the hot oil. Arrange the sausages on top.

4. Roast in the oven for about 20 minutes or until the sausages
    are brown on one side. Turn the sausages over and roast
    for a further 15 minutes or until vegetables are golden and
    tender and the sausages are crisp. Remove the sausages
    and leave to rest on a plate, loosely covered with foil to
    keep warm.

5. Turn the vegetables over, sprinkle with the cheese and
    cook in the oven for another 10 minutes until crisp and
    golden (see tip). Serve piping hot with the sausages.

Mary's Classic Tips:
* For serving children, the beetroot can be omitted, if you prefer.
* Keep in a simple layer so the vegetables stay crisp and do not
  become soggy.

Ham, Spinach & Goat's Cheese Pancakes

SERVES 6 / COOK TIME: 15–18 minutes

300g (11oz) baby spinach
100g (4oz) full-fat
  cream cheese
100g (4oz) full-fat soft goat's
  cheese (in a tub)
100g (4oz) good ham, diced
2 tsp grainy mustard
6 ready-to-eat pancakes
  (see tip)
30g (1oz) butter
30g (1oz) Parmesan cheese,
  finely grated
Salt and freshly ground
  black pepper

Prepare Ahead:
Can be assembled in the dish
up to 6 hours ahead, ready
for the oven.

Savoury pancakes are a treat for a weekend lunch and are remarkably reasonable to buy for something like this in a supermarket. This is a lovely, quick recipe, which can be adapted depending on what is in the fridge: add cooked bacon instead of ham, or chopped cherry tomatoes and a handful of chives.

1. Preheat the oven to 200°C/180°C fan/Gas 6.

2. Place the spinach in a large colander set over a bowl or the sink and pour over a kettleful of boiling water to wilt it. Leave to cool, then squeeze out any water and roughly chop (see tip).

3. Put the chopped spinach in a large bowl with the cream cheese, goat's cheese, ham and mustard, season with salt and pepper and mix well with a wooden spoon to combine.

4. Spread out one pancake on a board, spoon a sixth of the mixture in the top left quarter of the pancake and fold the pancake in half and then into quarters to encase the filling and make a triangular crêpe shape. Repeat using the remaining pancakes and filling.

5. Melt the butter in a small pan and use a little of the melted butter to grease an ovenproof dish. Arrange the pancakes in the dish, brush with the remaining butter and scatter over the cheese.

6. Bake in the oven for about 15–18 minutes until golden and bubbling. Serve hot with salad.

Mary's Classic Tips:
* If you would prefer to make your own pancakes, you could use the batter from the Individual Toads in the Hole on page 112.
* It's important that as much of the water as possible is removed from the spinach or it will make the filling soggy. To make sure it is dry, put the chopped spinach back into the colander and press the water out using a wooden spoon or the back of a ladle.

Medallions of Pork with Creamy Apple Sauce

SERVES 6 / COOK TIME: 50 minutes, plus resting

2 x 450g (1lb) pork fillets, trimmed of excess fat
1 tbsp sunflower oil
Salt and freshly ground black pepper

For the apple sauce
A knob of butter
1 onion, finely chopped
2 eating apples, peeled, cored and finely chopped
50ml (2fl oz) Calvados or brandy
200ml (7fl oz) chicken stock
200ml (7fl oz) full-fat crème fraîche
¼ tsp sugar
1 tbsp chopped thyme leaves, plus extra to garnish

For the garnish
A knob of butter
3 eating apples, peeled, cored and sliced into 6–8 wedges
¼ tsp sugar

Prepare Ahead:
The sauce can be made up to a day ahead.

Tender meat with a generous amount of creamy pouring sauce, delicately flavoured with apple and thyme.

1. Preheat the oven to 220°C/200°C fan/Gas 7.

2. Season the pork fillets with salt and pepper. Heat the oil in a large frying pan and brown in two batches over a high heat for 3–4 minutes until golden and sealed all over, including the ends.

3. Place in a roasting tin and roast in the oven for about 20 minutes until just cooked. Rest, loosely covered in foil, for about 10 minutes.

4. Meanwhile, make the sauce. Melt the butter in the same frying pan (wiped clean if needed), add the onion and apples and fry over a medium heat for 3–4 minutes. Cover with a lid and gently cook over a low heat for about 10 minutes until soft. Add the Calvados or brandy and boil for a few minutes to reduce by half, then pour in the stock and bring to the boil. Add the crème fraîche, plus any of the juices from the resting meat, season with salt and pepper and simmer for 3–4 minutes.

5. Add the sugar and chopped thyme leaves and blend until smooth, using either a hand blender (see tip), free-standing blender or food processor.

6. To make the garnish, melt the butter in a clean frying pan, add the apple slices and sugar and fry for 4–5 minutes until golden but still holding their shape.

7. Carve the pork and serve with the sauce (see tip) and apple slices, with extra thyme to garnish.

Mary's Classic Tips:
* If blending with a hand blender, you may want to transfer the sauce to a jug first so that it doesn't splatter everywhere.
* Gently reheat the sauce before serving, if necessary, and serve in a warmed jug.

Roast Loin of Pork with Crackling

SERVES 6 / COOK TIME: 1½ hours

2 tbsp sunflower oil
1.5kg (3lb) loin of pork,
  boned and rolled, skin
  scored (see tip)
A large pinch of salt
2 large onions, sliced

For the gravy
50g (2oz) butter
3 tbsp plain flour
200ml (7fl oz) white wine
300ml (10fl oz) hot
  chicken stock
2 tsp redcurrant jelly
A dash of Worcestershire sauce

Prepare Ahead:
Any leftovers are delicious
served cold the next day.

Mary's Classic Tips:
* If you're buying your pork
  from a butcher, ask them to
  score the skin for you with
  their super-sharp knives.
  Plenty of scored lines
  means more surface area to
  get golden and crisp.
* If the pork skin is already
  quite crispy when it comes
  out of the oven, arrange the
  crackling strips on the
  baking tray with the paler,
  fattier side upwards to let
  this side crisp more.

Loin pork is a delicious, moist cut and easy to carve. Good crackling is all about the preparation before it goes into the oven: the oil will crisp the skin and the salt draws out extra moisture, drying it out and of course adding flavour. I have taken the crackling off the joint and cut into strips to get it very crisp.

1. Preheat the oven to 220°C/200°C fan/Gas 7, then add half the sunflower oil to a roasting tin and place in the oven to heat up.

2. Dab the skin of the pork with kitchen paper, to remove any moisture, then rub the rest of the sunflower oil and a large pinch of salt into the skin. Remove the roasting tin from the oven, add the sliced onions and toss in the hot oil. Push the onions into the centre of the tin to make a little pile and sit the pork on top.

3. Roast in the oven for about 1 hour 20 minutes or until the juices run clear and the skin of the pork is golden and nearly crisp.

4. Remove from the oven. Using a small sharp knife, remove the crackling from the loin in one piece. Use a sharp pair of scissors to snip the crackling into long, thin strips. Arrange the strips on a baking tray lined with baking paper and place in the oven to crisp up for about 5–10 minutes, turning halfway through, until golden and crisp all over (see tip). Meanwhile, cover the pork with foil and leave to rest while you make the gravy.

5. Discard the onions. Add the butter, melt in the flour to the fat in the tin and stir into a roux over a medium heat. Pour in the wine and stock, then bring to the boil and stir until the gravy has thickened and reduced by a third. Stir in the redcurrant jelly so that it dissolves, and add the Worcestershire sauce. Strain through a fine sieve into a warmed jug.

6. Serve slices of pork with pieces of crunchy crackling and the gravy and, if you like, with some apple sauce on the side.

Jumbo Bangers with Cheesy Mash

SERVES 4–6 / COOK TIME: 35-45 minutes

A knob of butter, plus extra
   for greasing
8 jumbo sausages
   (about 100g/4oz each)
550g (1¼lb) potatoes, peeled
   and diced
2 tbsp milk
1 tbsp grainy mustard
50g (2oz) mature Cheddar
   cheese, grated
Salt

Prepare Ahead:
Can be arranged in the
dish, ready for the oven,
up to 6 hours ahead.

Classic bangers and mash, but presented in a different way. If the kids aren't very keen on grainy mustard, leave it out, or use less.

1. Preheat the oven to 200°C/180°C fan/Gas 6, then line a roasting tin with baking paper and grease a large ovenproof dish with butter (see tip).

2. Place the sausages in the lined roasting tin and bake in the oven for about 20–25 minutes, turning halfway through, until cooked and lightly golden (see tip). Alternatively, fry in a pan over a medium heat for about 10–15 minutes on the hob. Once cooked, leave until cool enough to handle.

3. Meanwhile, place the potatoes in a saucepan of cold salted water. Cover with a lid, bring to the boil and cook for about 15 minutes or until tender. Drain well, then mash. Add the butter, milk and mustard and mix together well, beating with a wooden spoon or spatula. Season with salt and pepper.

4. Slice each sausage lengthways, cutting three-quarters of the way through and then opening out like a butterfly. Use a dessertspoon to fill each sausage with mashed potato along its length.

5. Arrange in the prepared ovenproof dish, sprinkle the cheese on top and bake in the oven for about 15–20 minutes until golden.

Mary's Classic Tips:
* Cooking the filled sausages in the ovenproof dish means they can be served straight from the oven to the table, rather than in the roasting tin. Greasing is necessary to stop the sausages sticking to the dish and tearing when you lift them out. It also makes it easier to lift off any loose bits of crispy, melted cheese for extra crunchy topping.
* Don't worry if the sausages aren't too darkly coloured when they come out of the oven at this stage. Once filled, they will go back in the oven and cook further.

Spicy Chorizo Penne Pasta

SERVES 4 / COOK TIME: 12 minutes

1 x 120g packet of thinly
   sliced chorizo, snipped
   into thin pieces
300g (11oz) penne pasta
2 tbsp olive oil
2 large banana shallots, sliced
2 large garlic cloves, crushed
½ fresh red chilli, deseeded
   and diced
½ tsp sugar
175ml (6fl oz) white wine
1 small bunch of parsley,
   chopped
1 small bunch of basil,
   chopped
Juice of ½ lemon
75g (3oz) Parmesan cheese,
   finely grated
Salt and freshly ground
   black pepper

Prepare Ahead:
The chorizo can be fried
in advance.

I love penne pasta as it collects all the flavours and this has a bit of a kick to it. A really quick, tasty meal, perfect when you've got hungry mouths to feed in a hurry.

1. Heat a frying pan until hot. Add the chorizo and dry-fry for 2–3 minutes until crisp (you will need to do this in batches), then set aside on a plate.

2. Cook the pasta in boiling salted water according to the packet instructions.

3. While the pasta is cooking, heat the oil in the frying pan. Add the shallots, garlic, chilli and sugar and fry over a medium heat for 3–4 minutes until soft. Pour in the wine, bring to a simmer and cook until reduced by a third.

4. Drain the pasta, reserving 75ml (3fl oz) of the cooking water. Tip the pasta into the frying pan and toss together with the herbs and chopped chorizo. Add the reserved pasta water to make a nice coating consistency.

5. Add the lemon juice and season well with salt and pepper, remove from the heat and stir through the Parmesan until melted. Serve at once.

Mary's Classic Tip:
* The chorizo for this recipe needs to be wafer thin, like bacon; it is much nicer to eat than the thick, chunky chorizo pieces.

Individual Toads in the Hole with Onion Gravy

SERVES 4–8 / COOK TIME: 35–40 minutes

8 sausages
100g (4oz) plain flour
3 eggs
150ml (5fl oz) milk
3 tbsp sunflower oil

For the onion gravy
1 tbsp sunflower oil
1 onion, very thinly sliced
2 tbsp plain flour
450ml (15fl oz) beef stock
1 tsp soy sauce
1 tsp Worcestershire sauce
½ tsp balsamic vinegar
A few drops of
   gravy browning

Prepare Ahead:
The batter can be made up to 8 hours ahead. The onion gravy can be made up to day in advance.

If you don't have Yorkshire pudding tins, you could make one large toad in the hole instead in a roasting tin or ovenproof dish – it will take 30–35 minutes to cook.

1. You will need two four-hole Yorkshire pudding tins. Preheat the oven to 220°C/200°C fan/Gas 7.

2. Put the sausages in a shallow roasting tin and roast in the oven for 20 minutes until browned on one side.

3. Measure the flour into a bowl. Make a well in the centre, add the eggs and beat with a whisk, gradually combining to make a paste, then slowly add the milk until you have a smooth, fairly runny batter (see tip).

4. Pour 1 teaspoon of oil into the base of each mould and heat until piping hot. Divide the batter into the tins, pouring into the oil. Place a sausage, browned side down, in the middle of each and bake for 15–18 minutes until risen and golden.

5. Meanwhile to make the gravy, heat the oil in a saucepan and fry the onion over a high heat for 1–2 minutes. Lower the heat, cover with a lid and cook for 15 minutes until softened. Add the flour, stirring it in for 30 seconds, then gradually blend in the stock, mixing until smooth and lump-free (see tip). Bring to the boil, then add the soy sauce, Worcestershire sauce, vinegar and gravy browning.

6. Serve the toads piping hot with the onion gravy.

Mary's Classic Tips:
* Once the batter is made, put it into a jug to make it easier to pour out into the pudding tins later.
* It's important to gradually blend the stock into the flour for the onion gravy to get a really smooth paste. It's trickier to check if the lumps here are flour or onion pieces, so give it a really good mix to make sure no doughy lumps remain.

Pork Sichuan Noodles

SERVES 4–6 / COOK TIME: 10 minutes

200g (7oz) vermicelli noodles
2 tbsp olive oil
8 spring onions, sliced
1 large carrot, peeled and
    finely diced
2 celery sticks, finely diced
2 garlic cloves, crushed
½ fresh red chilli, deseeded
    (optional) and finely diced
500g (1lb 2oz) lean
    minced pork
2 tsp Chinese five
    spice powder
3 tbsp hoisin sauce
2 tbsp soy sauce
Juice of 1 lime
1 small bunch of coriander,
    chopped
Salt and freshly ground
    black pepper
50g (2oz) unsalted cashew
    nuts, chopped, to serve
    (see tip)

Light and healthy, this type of cooking is a real classic of our time. These noodles are very fragrant tasting and colourful, with plenty of crunch. Perfect to whip up for a weekday meal or a tasty alternative to a weekend takeaway.

1. Cook the noodles in boiling salted water according to the packet instructions. Drain and run under cold water, then snip in half and set aside.

2. Meanwhile, heat the oil in pan or wok, add the spring onions, carrot, celery, garlic and chilli and stir-fry over a medium-high heat for 3–4 minutes.

3. Add the minced pork and fry for about 2–3 minutes until golden brown all over, breaking the mince up with two wooden spoons.

4. Sprinkle over the five spice and fry for 2–3 minutes. Add the hoisin sauce, soy sauce and lime juice. Season with salt and black pepper and toss over a high heat until everything is coated and glossy. Add the noodles and coriander and toss to combine.

5. Transfer to a warmed serving bowl and sprinkle with the nuts to serve.

Mary's Classic Tip:
* Toast the cashew nuts for more flavour, if you prefer. Dry-fry in a pan over a high heat for a few minutes, keeping a careful eye on them to make sure they don't burn.

Extra Trimmed Rack of Lamb with Orange & Thyme Sauce

SERVES 4–6 / MARINATE: A minimum of 2 hours / COOK TIME: 30 minutes, plus resting

2 racks of lamb, extra trimmed and chine bone removed (about 600g/1lb 5oz each – see tip)

For the marinade
2 tbsp orange marmalade
2 garlic cloves, crushed
2 tbsp olive oil
1 tbsp chopped thyme leaves

For the sauce
200ml (7fl oz) full-fat crème fraîche
2 tsp orange marmalade
3 tbsp orange juice from a carton
2 tsp chopped thyme leaves
Salt and freshly ground black pepper

Prepare Ahead:
Marinate the lamb up to a day ahead.

Freeze:
The marinated lamb can be frozen. (The sauce is not suitable for freezing.)

Rack of lamb is a simple, quick roast to do – more suited to entertaining than a Sunday roast. This makes such a quick, impressive meal and the orange thyme sauce really gives it zing.

1. Mix the marinade ingredients together in a bowl. Spread over the lamb, then place in a freezer bag and massage all the flavours into the meat. Leave to marinate in the fridge for a minimum of 2 hours.

2. When you are ready to cook, preheat the oven to 220°C/200°C fan/Gas 7.

3. Heat a non-stick frying pan until piping hot. Remove the lamb from the marinade and brown over a high heat on all sides (see tip), for 3–4 minutes until golden. Place the racks in a roasting tin, sitting each one on its end, fat side up, with the bones interlinked and facing the middle.

4. Roast for 18 minutes for pink, 20–22 for well done, or until golden on the outside but still pink in the middle. Leave to rest for 5 minutes while you make the sauce.

5. Add the crème fraîche, marmalade and any leftover marinade to the roasting tin, together with enough orange juice to make the sauce a good pouring consistency. Stir in any juices from the resting meat for extra flavour. Whisk and bring to the boil, reduce a little, season to taste and add the thyme leaves.

6. Carve the lamb between the bones into cutlets and serve with the orange and thyme sauce.

Mary's Classic Tips:
* Racks of lamb from the supermarket may be smaller in size and therefore take less time to roast.
* Remember to brown the ends of each rack of lamb so that all the exposed meat is seared.

Irish Stew

SERVES 6–8 / COOK TIME: 2–2½ hours, plus resting

2 tbsp plain flour

1kg (2lb 3oz) neck fillet of lamb, diced into 2cm (¾in) cubes (see tip)

2–3 tbsp oil

2 onions, sliced

2 celery sticks, sliced

3 medium carrots, peeled and sliced

2 bay leaves

1 tbsp chopped thyme leaves

600ml (1 pint) chicken or lamb stock

750g (1¾lb) floury potatoes (such as Maris Piper), peeled and cut into slices about 1cm (½in) thick

Salt and freshly ground black pepper

Prepare Ahead:
Can be assembled up to 8 hours ahead, making sure that the potato is covered with stock so that it does not dry out or discolour.

Full of flavour and one of the original one-pot dishes. I like to use the neck fillet, rather than the scrag end and middle neck joints on the bone, which is traditional. I also like to thicken the stock a little by tossing the meat in seasoned flour. The result is really tender, melt-in-the-mouth lamb with flavoursome gravy.

1. Preheat the oven to 180°C/160°C Fan/Gas 4.

2. Season the flour and then toss in the lamb. Heat some of the oil in a wide-based flameproof, ovenproof casserole dish with a lid, then fry in batches over a high heat for 4–6 minutes until golden. Add oil as needed and remove each batch with a slotted spoon to set aside while you cook the rest.

3. Add a little more oil to the pan, then tip in the onions, celery and carrots and fry over a medium-high heat for 4–5 minutes. Add the bay leaves and thyme and scatter the browned lamb over the top. Pour over the stock and bring to the boil.

4. Reduce the heat and arrange the potatoes on top. Season with salt and pepper as you layer the potato slices, gently pressing down so the liquid rises to cover them.

5. Cover with the lid and carefully transfer to the oven to cook for 1½–2 hours (see tip) or until tender. Increase the oven temperature to 200°C/180°C fan/Gas 6, remove the lid and cook 8–10 minutes more until the potatoes are golden.

6. Allow to stand for 5 minutes and remove the bay leaves before serving with a leafy green vegetable, such as chard or cabbage.

Mary's Classic Tips:
* Ask your butcher to give you the bones from the filleted neck – perfect for making stock. Roast the bones for a fuller flavour, then cover with water and simmer with herbs and chopped vegetables for an hour. Freeze to use when you next make stew.
* Check the stew after 1½ hours – you don't want it to dry out, particularly as it will be cooked for another 8–10 minutes.

Lamb Shanks with Winter Vegetables

SERVES 6 / COOK TIME: 4½ hours

3 tbsp oil
6 small lamb shanks
(300–400g/11–14oz each)
(see tip)
3 large carrots, peeled and
cut into large dice
2 celery sticks, sliced
2 onions, sliced
2 fat garlic cloves, crushed
50g (2oz) plain flour
300ml (10fl oz) red wine
300ml (10fl oz) beef stock
2 tbsp tomato purée
Leaves from 3 sprigs of
rosemary, finely chopped
2 bay leaves
2 tbsp redcurrant jelly
A knob of butter
250g (9oz) chestnut
mushrooms, sliced
Salt and freshly ground
black pepper
2 tbsp chopped parsley,
to garnish

Good English flavours with a lovely, rich sauce. I like to use very small lamb shanks or fore shanks as I find a whole shank too much to eat and imposing on the plate, but it's up to you. Serve with a green leafy winter vegetable such as kale to make the ultimate warming winter meal, perfect for those stay-indoors days.

1. You will need a 4-litre (7-pint) deep flameproof and ovenproof casserole dish with a lid. Preheat the oven to 160°C/140°C fan/Gas 3.

2. Heat 1 tablespoon of the oil in the casserole dish (see tip). Fry the lamb on all sides over a high heat until golden. You will need to do this in two batches. The shanks are a tricky shape, so keep turning in the oil to brown them – it will take around 10 minutes per batch. Once they are browned, set the shanks aside on a plate.

3. Add the remaining oil to the dish, along with the carrots, celery, onions and garlic, and fry over a high heat for about 4 minutes.

4. Measure the flour into a large bowl and gradually stir in the wine and the stock, mixing until smooth.

5. Add the tomato purée to the vegetables in the dish and pour in the stock mixture, stirring over a high heat until it comes to the boil and is smooth and thickened. Season with salt and pepper and stir in the rosemary, bay leaves and redcurrant jelly.

Continued overleaf →

6. Add the lamb shanks and bring to the boil. Cover with the lid and transfer to the oven to cook for 4 hours or until the lamb is tender and the meat falls off the bone. Check the dish halfway through cooking and push any exposed lamb shanks into the liquid.

7. Shortly before the lamb is ready, melt the butter in a frying pan, add the mushrooms and fry over a medium heat for 2–3 minutes. Add the mushrooms to the casserole and remove the bay leaves. Scatter with the chopped parsley and serve piping hot with mash (see page 177).

Prepare Ahead:
Can be made up to 2 days ahead and reheated.

Freeze:
This dish freezes well.

Mary's Classic Tips:
* If fore shanks are not available, ask your butcher for shoulder shanks, which are often smaller than the standard kind.
* If your casserole dish is not flameproof, use a large, deep frying pan for the hob cooking and transfer everything to the casserole dish for cooking in the oven.

Moussaka

SERVES 6–8 / COOK TIME: 2 hours–2 hours 10 minutes

1kg (2lb 3oz) lean
   minced lamb
2 onions, finely chopped
2 celery sticks, finely diced
3 garlic cloves, crushed
2 tbsp tomato purée
2 tbsp plain flour
200ml (7fl oz) red wine
2 x 400g tins of
   chopped tomatoes
1 tbsp chopped marjoram
2 tbsp chopped mint
4 medium aubergines
   (about 300g/11oz each),
   cut into slices about 1cm
   (½in) thick
3 tbsp olive oil
500g (1lb 2oz) potatoes,
   peeled and cut into slices
   about 1cm (½in) thick
Salt and freshly ground
   black pepper

For the cheese sauce
50g (2oz) butter
50g (2oz) plain flour
450ml (15fl oz) hot milk
1 tsp Dijon mustard
150g (5oz) Cheddar cheese,
   grated
1 large egg, beaten

Some classic moussakas have sliced potato and some do not – it depends on the heritage of the recipe; we personally like it with the potato. This takes quite a long time to prepare/cook, but the slow-cooking of the lamb does produce lovely, tender mince.

1. You will need a 2-litre (3½-pint) deep ovenproof dish. Preheat the oven to 160°C/140°C fan/Gas 3.

2. Heat a large, deep non-stick ovenproof frying pan until hot (see tip). Add the minced lamb and fry over a high heat for 3–4 minutes until browned. Spoon the mince into a large bowl and remove all but 1 tablespoon of fat from the pan. Add the onions, celery and garlic and fry for 3–4 minutes over a medium heat, then return the lamb to the pan and toss together.

3. Add the tomato purée and flour and stir for 30 seconds. Add the wine, tomatoes and marjoram, cover with a lid and bring to the boil, then transfer to the oven to cook for 1 hour or until tender. Remove from the oven, season with salt and pepper and add the mint. Spoon the lamb into the ovenproof dish and set aside.

4. Increase the oven temperature to 200°C/180°C fan/Gas 6. Arrange the aubergine slices in a single layer on two large baking sheets. Drizzle with the olive oil and season with salt and pepper. Roast in the oven for about 25–30 minutes until golden brown and tender, then set aside.

Prepare Ahead:
Can be assembled up to
6 hours ahead and baked in
the oven to serve.

....

Freeze:
Freezes well.

5. Meanwhile, place the potatoes in a pan of boiling salted water, bring back up to the boil and cook for about 4 minutes until just soft but still holding their shape. Carefully tip into a colander to drain.

6. To make the cheese sauce, melt the butter in a saucepan over a medium heat. Add the flour and stir over the heat for 30 seconds. Blend in the hot milk, adding it gradually and whisking until you have a smooth sauce. Season with salt and pepper, add the mustard and three-quarters of the cheese. Remove from the heat and allow to stand for 5 minutes before adding the beaten egg. Mix together well.

7. Arrange the potatoes over the mince, then arrange the aubergine in a neat layer on top. Pour over the sauce, making sure it spreads out to the edges, and sprinkle with the remaining cheese. Place on a baking sheet and bake in the oven for 25–30 minutes (see tip) until golden and bubbling.

Mary's Classic Tips:
* The frying pan used to brown the mince needs to be ovenproof as it goes in the oven to cook for an hour. If your frying pan isn't ovenproof, with a non-metal handle, then use a cast-iron casserole dish or other hob-to-oven pan for cooking the mince.
* If assembling in advance and cooking from cold, bake for 35–45 minutes.

Butterflied Leg of Lamb with Mint Raita

SERVES 6 / MARINATE: A minimum of 2 hours / COOK TIME: 25 minutes, plus resting

2kg (4¼lb) leg of lamb, butterflied and fat removed (see tip)
12 flatbreads or tortillas

For the marinade
Juice and finely grated zest of 1½ lemons
1 tbsp runny honey
1 tbsp ground coriander
1 tbsp ground cumin
2 tbsp olive oil
Salt and freshly ground black pepper

For the raita
500g (1lb 2oz) natural yoghurt
¼ large cucumber, deseeded (see tip), finely chopped
2 heaped tbsp chopped mint
2 heaped tbsp chopped dill
2 tsp ground cumin
Grated zest of ½ lemon
2 pickled cucumber spears with dill (from a jar), finely chopped

Prepare Ahead:
The lamb can be marinated overnight. Roast up to 8 hours ahead if serving cold. Make the raita up to 3 days ahead and store in the fridge.

Freeze:
The lamb can be frozen in the marinade.

The marinade gives the crust of the meat a good colour and lots of flavour and the raita is fresh and cooling. Serve with a salad to give some extra crunch and the hummus on page 16 too if liked. This would work perfectly on the BBQ – it's a lovely summer dish. Sear over a high heat, then cook for 15–20 minutes each side on a medium heat over a cooler part of the barbecue.

1. Place the lamb on a board so that it is spread out like a butterfly. Lay a sheet of cling film on the top and bash the thickest parts of the meat, with a meat mallet, so the lamb is a fairly even thickness throughout.

2. Place the lamb in a large dish or freezer bag. Mix together all the ingredients for the marinade in a bowl, season generously with salt and pepper and pour over the lamb. Rub into the meat to coat, then cover the dish (if using) and transfer to the fridge to marinate for a minimum of 2 hours.

3. In a separate bowl, mix together all the ingredients for the raita and season with a good pinch of salt.

4. Shortly before you are ready to cook the lamb, preheat the oven to 200°C/180°C fan/Gas 6.

5. Place a large ovenproof frying pan over a high heat and add the lamb. Brown on one side for 5 minutes, then transfer to the oven to cook for about 20 minutes or until browned all over and still pink in the middle. Transfer to a board, cover in foil and leave to rest for about 15 minutes before carving.

6. Warm the flatbreads according to the packet instructions, then slice the meat and serve with the warmed flatbreads and a dollop of mint raita.

Mary's Classic Tips:
* Ask your butcher to remove the leg bone to butterfly the lamb, and save it to make stock.
* Remove the seeds from the cucumber with a teaspoon, or a melon baller if you have one.

Stuffed Roast Leg of Lamb with Mushrooms

SERVES 6 / COOK TIME: 1½ hours, plus resting

1 x 1.8kg (4lb) leg of lamb, tunnel boned (see tip)
Olive oil, for rubbing into the lamb
2 large sprigs of rosemary

For the mushroom stuffing
A knob of butter
2 shallots, chopped
175g (6oz) button mushrooms, chopped
2 fat garlic cloves, crushed
1 large bunch of flat-leaf parsley, roughly chopped
1 egg yolk, beaten
2 tbsp fresh white breadcrumbs
Salt and freshly ground black pepper

For the gravy
1 tbsp plain flour
450ml (15fl oz) beef or chicken stock
1 tbsp Worcestershire sauce
1 tbsp redcurrant jelly

Prepare Ahead:
The leg can be stuffed up to 2 days ahead.

Freeze:
The stuffed leg can be frozen uncooked.

A lovely way to add interest to a leg of lamb. Many butchers and supermarkets sell part-boned legs of lamb, which saves on the cooking time. No need to tie up the meat before cooking to hold the stuffing, the tunnel-boned cavity keeps it all neatly in place.

1. Preheat the oven to 220°C/200°C fan/Gas 7.

2. To make the stuffing, melt the butter in a pan over a medium heat and fry the shallots for 2–3 minutes. Add the mushrooms and garlic and fry for 2 minutes until just cooked. Tip into a bowl, add parsley, yolk and breadcrumbs, season and mix.

3. Spoon the mushroom filling into the 'tunnel' in the leg of lamb, pushing it in well. Rub the lamb with olive oil and season with pepper. Place the rosemary sprigs in the bottom of a roasting tin and sit the lamb on top.

4. Roast for 20 minutes. Reduce the temperature to 200°C/180°C fan/Gas 6 and cook for another hour (or 15 minutes per 450g/1lb – see tip). Remove the joint from the oven and transfer to a board to rest while you make the gravy.

5. Skim the surplus fat from the roasting tin with a spoon, leaving about 1 tablespoon in the tin. Place over a medium heat, sprinkle in the flour and stir well, scraping up any sediment and juices in the bottom of the tin. Stir in the stock, Worcestershire sauce and redcurrant jelly, season and bring to the boil, stirring. Boil for 2–3 minutes, then strain.

6. Carve the stuffed lamb and serve with the gravy.

Mary's Classic Tips:
* Ask your butcher to remove the main leg bone from the leg of lamb. To tunnel bone the lamb yourself, use a sharp knife to scrape along the side of the bone. Once you reach the ball and socket joint, cut through the cartilage and discard the bone; you can leave the knuckle end in the leg to keep the shape.
* If you like your lamb well done, cook for 20 minutes per 450g/lb after reducing the oven temperature.

Cannon of Lamb with Minted Spring Vegetables

SERVES 6 / COOK TIME: 20–25 minutes, plus resting

2 cannons of lamb, well
trimmed of any fat and
skin (see tip)
1 tbsp olive oil
2 sprigs of rosemary
250g (9oz) asparagus spears,
woody ends snapped off
250g (9oz) frozen baby
broad beans
250g (9oz) frozen petits pois

For the dressing
3 spring onions, finely chopped
1 garlic clove, crushed
2 tbsp chopped mint
1 tbsp grainy mustard
1 tbsp white wine vinegar
150ml (5fl oz) good olive oil
Juice of ½ lemon
1 heaped tsp sugar
Salt and freshly ground
black pepper

Mary's Classic Tips:
* Ask your butcher to trim
  the lamb for you, or if you
  are buying from a
  supermarket, look for 'loin
  of lamb', as this cut is
  sometimes labelled.
* It's best to cook the broad
  beans separately to keep
  their bright colour and
  prevent them going grey
  through overcooking.

Cannon is the very tender fillet loin of lamb, with a short cooking time and such a treat. Dress the vegetables just before serving to save them discolouring. This goes very well with the garlicky roast potatoes on page 173.

1. You will need six little jugs (or one big one) for the dressing. Preheat the oven to 220°C/200°C fan/Gas 7.

2. To make the dressing, place all of the dressing ingredients in a jug or bowl, season with salt and pepper and mix to combine.

3. Heat a frying pan until hot and add the oil. Season the lamb with salt and pepper and brown quickly over a high heat for 2–3 minutes until golden and sealed on all sides. Place the rosemary sprigs on a baking tray and sit a cannon of lamb on top of each sprig.

4. Roast in the oven for 8 minutes for pink, 12 for well done, then place on a warmed plate, cover with foil and leave to rest for 5 minutes.

5. Meanwhile, cut the tips off the asparagus and slice the stems into 1cm (½in) lengths. Place the broad beans in a saucepan of boiling water and cook for 3 minutes. Using a slotted spoon, transfer the beans to a warmed bowl (see tip) and bring the water in the pan back up to the boil. Tip in the asparagus pieces and the petits pois and cook for 4 minutes, then drain and add to the broad beans.

6. Gently warm the dressing in a small saucepan, then pour into the six little jugs or single big jug.

7. Divide the vegetables among individual plates. Carve each cannon into slices and arrange next to the vegetables. Spoon a little dressing over the lamb and serve the rest on the side. Pour over the rest of the dressing just before serving.

Beef Burgers with Beetroot & Carrot Slaw

MAKES 6 burgers / COOK TIME: 6–8 minutes per batch

For the burgers
500g (1lb 2oz) lean
    minced beef
50g (2oz) fresh white
    breadcrumbs
1 small onion, finely chopped
1 tbsp chopped marjoram
3 tbsp chopped parsley
2 tsp Dijon mustard
1 tbsp sun-dried tomato paste
1 egg yolk
2 tbsp oil, for frying
Salt and freshly ground
    black pepper

For the slaw
4 tbsp full-fat mayonnaise
2 tsp Dijon mustard
1 tbsp hot horseradish sauce
A squeeze of lemon juice
1 tsp sugar
1 large carrot, peeled and
    coarsely grated
150g (5oz) raw beetroot,
    peeled and coarsely grated
2 celery sticks, very finely
    chopped
2 spring onions, chopped
3 tbsp chopped parsley

To serve
6 burger or brioche buns
1 Little Gem lettuce, shredded
2 large beefsteak tomatoes,
    each cut into 6 slices
6 large sweet dill
    cucumbers, sliced

Nothing nicer than a burger when it is full of flavour and cooked quickly – overcooked they become tough and chewy.

1. First make the slaw. Measure the mayonnaise, mustard and horseradish sauce into a bowl, add the lemon juice and sugar, season and stir to combine. Tip in the carrot, beetroot, celery, spring onions and parsley and stir until coated in the sauce. Season to taste and add more lemon juice if required. Set aside to allow the flavours to develop.

2. To make the burgers, place all the ingredients (except the oil) in a large bowl, season and mix with your hands until combined. Shape into six fairly flat burgers – about 1cm (½in) thick and 9cm (3½in) in diameter is ideal (see tip). Chill in the fridge until needed.

3. Heat the oil in a large frying pan until piping hot, then fry the burgers, in batches, over a high heat for 3–4 minutes on each side until browned and just cooked through.

4. Meanwhile, slice the buns in half and toast the flat side in a preheated griddle pan, or simply grill or toast the buns on one side. Top the flat side with some lettuce, followed by a slice or two of tomato, the burger and some cucumber slices. Add any sauces or chutney of your choice, then place the other half of each bun on top and serve with the slaw on the side.

Prepare Ahead:
The burgers can be prepared (but not cooked) up to a day ahead.

Freeze:
The burgers freeze well uncooked; place pieces of greaseproof paper between them so they can easily be separated once frozen.

Mary's Classic Tip:
* Wear rubber gloves to stop the beetroot from staining your hands bright pink! And grate on to a plate rather than a chopping board, which is a less absorbent surface and easier to wash.

Sirloin Steaks with Béarnaise Sauce

SERVES 4 / COOK TIME: 30 minutes, plus resting

4 x 225g (8oz) sirloin steaks
Oil, for frying

For the Béarnaise sauce
250g (9oz) butter
4 tbsp white wine vinegar
3 shallots, finely chopped
5 sprigs of tarragon
Juice of ½ lemon
4 egg yolks, beaten
Salt and freshly ground
    black pepper

....

Prepare Ahead:
The sauce can be made up to
a day ahead (see tip).

Don't be scared of cooking steak; it's easy, simple and loved by all meat eaters. This is a lovely classic dish, which is achievable at home. The old-school Béarnaise sauce is great with the steak – all you need is a hand whisk, a heatproof bowl and a steady hand. As long as the melted butter is added slowly and gradually with plenty of whisking throughout, you will remain in control of the sauce as it thickens to your preferred texture.

1. First make the Béarnaise sauce. Melt the butter in a saucepan over a low heat then set aside to cool.

2. Place the vinegar and shallots in a small saucepan. Strip the leaves from the tarragon sprigs, then chop the leaves and set aside. Add the stalks to the pan.

3. Bring the vinegar mixture to the boil and reduce by half. Strain into a large heatproof bowl; you will need just 2 tablespoons of the reduced liquid. Add the lemon juice and egg yolks.

4. Put the bowl over a saucepan of simmering water and whisk over a gentle heat until the sauce is thickened and a 'coating' consistency (see tip). Remove from the heat and slowly add the melted butter, whisking all the time, until you have a thick glossy sauce (see tip). Season with salt and pepper and add the chopped tarragon leaves.

Continued overleaf →

5. Heat a frying pan or griddle pan until piping butter. Rub a little oil on to each side of the steaks and season with salt and pepper. Fry two steaks at a time over a high heat for 2–3 minutes on each side for rare or 3–4 minutes for medium, depending on your preference. Remove from the pan and allow to rest for 5 minutes.

6. Serve the steaks in one piece or in slices with the warm sauce.

Mary's Classic Tips:
* If making the sauce ahead, store in the bowl in the fridge overnight with a layer of cling film covering the sauce so that it touches the surface, then gently warm through by whisking over a saucepan of simmering water.
* A 'coating' consistency is reached when the sauce coats the back of a spoon without running off quickly.
* When whisking in the melted butter, stand the mixing bowl on a damp tea towel or other cloth to stop it moving around on the work surface. This means you have a hand free for pouring in the melted butter. If it helps, put the melted butter in a jug to make it easier to add gradually.

Beef Stroganoff

SERVES 4–6 / COOK TIME: 16–20 minutes

2 tbsp sunflower oil
650g (1lb 7oz) fillet of beef,
    sliced across the grain into
    thin strips about 1cm (½in)
    thick (see tip)
A large knob of butter
1 large onion, thinly sliced
2 garlic cloves, crushed
1½ tbsp tomato purée
1 heaped tsp paprika
75ml (3fl oz) brandy
200ml (7fl oz) beef stock
300ml (10fl oz) double cream
2 tsp Dijon mustard
1 tbsp Worcestershire sauce
1 tsp muscovado sugar
Salt and freshly ground
    black pepper

To serve
4–6 gherkins, chopped
2 tbsp chopped parsley

Tender strips of prime beef in a classic sauce. So quick and easy, it makes a speedy but special meal. The gherkins make a tasty topping.

1. Heat a large frying pan until hot, then add the oil. Season the beef well with salt and pepper and then fry in two batches over a high heat for 1–2 minutes, stirring occasionally, until golden, but not fully cooked. Set each batch aside on a plate as it is cooked.

2. Melt the butter in the frying pan, then add the onion and fry over a medium heat for about 10 minutes until softened. Add the garlic and fry for 30 seconds, then add the tomato purée and paprika and cook for a few more seconds before pouring in the brandy. Allow to bubble away over the heat, then add the stock, bring back up to the boil and cook for 2–3 minutes to reduce by a third.

3. Add the cream, mustard, Worcestershire sauce and sugar, along with any juices from the beef on the plate. Stir for 2–3 minutes until the sauce has thickened slightly, then season well with salt and pepper.

4. Add the beef and gently simmer for 4–5 minutes until heated through. Sprinkle over the chopped gherkins and parsley and serve with boiled rice.

Mary's Classic Tip:
* As the fillet of beef is cut into strips for this recipe, rather than cooked in one piece, why not ask your butcher for the tail pieces or offcuts; he may be able to offer a lower price.

Fillet of Beef with Horseradish & Parsley Sauce

SERVES 6–8 / COOK TIME: 32 minutes, plus resting

1.8kg (4lb) whole fillet of beef
(cut from the centre)
Oil, for rubbing into the meat
A knob of butter
Salt and freshly ground
black pepper

For the horseradish sauce
200ml (7fl oz) full-fat
crème fraîche
4 tbsp hot horseradish sauce
2 tbsp light mayonnaise
5 tbsp chopped parsley

Prepare Ahead:
To serve hot, brown the beef
up to a day ahead and roast
to serve. To serve cold, roast
up to 2 days ahead. Leave
uncut until just before
serving. The horseradish
sauce can be made up to
3 days ahead and stored in
the fridge.

My absolute classic for any party or entertaining. The joy of beef is seeing it pink; however, if you slice it ahead the meat surface will turn grey half an hour or so after being exposed to the air, so carve at the last minute.

1. Preheat the oven to 220°C/200°C fan/Gas 7.

2. Season the beef with salt and pepper and rub a little oil into the meat. Heat a large frying pan until very hot and brown the fillet quickly on all sides (see tip).

3. Transfer the fillet to a small roasting tin, spread with the butter and roast in the oven for about 32 minutes for medium rare (or 8 minutes per 450g/1lb). If the fillet is a slim long piece, roast only for 22 minutes. Remove from the oven and allow to rest for 10–15 minutes.

4. To make the sauce, mix all the ingredients together in a bowl and season with salt and pepper.

5. Carve the meat into thin slices and serve with the sauce.

Mary's Classic Tip:
* Use tongs or a pair of sturdy forks to turn the beef while it's browning in the frying pan; it's a large, heavy piece of meat that needs lifting carefully.

Spaghetti Meatballs

SERVES 8 / COOK TIME: 30 minutes

400g (14oz) lean minced beef
50g (2oz) fresh breadcrumbs
   or rolled oats
1 egg, beaten
2 tbsp chopped parsley
100g (4oz) Parmesan cheese,
   finely grated
1–2 tbsp olive oil
400g (14oz) spaghetti
Salt and freshly ground
   black pepper

For the tomato sauce
1 tbsp olive oil
1 onion, finely chopped
2 garlic cloves, crushed
1 litre (1¾ pints) passata
1 tbsp sun-dried
   tomato paste
1 tsp sugar

Prepare Ahead:
The meatballs and the
sauce can be made up to
12 hours ahead.

Freeze:
The uncooked meatballs
freeze well: place in a
freezer-proof container so
that they keep their shape
while freezing.

A great family favourite, especially with children, which is easy to eat and full of flavour. Originally a popular Swedish classic, but loved worldwide now.

1. Place the beef in a bowl with the breadcrumbs, egg, parsley and half the cheese. Season and mix together with your hands. Shape into 40 even-sized meatballs.

2. Heat 1 tablespoon of the oil in large frying pan and fry the meatballs in batches over a high heat for 3–4 minutes on each side until golden all over (see tips). Fry the meatballs in batches, if needed, adding more oil if the pan gets too dry. Carefully remove with tongs or fork and spoon and set aside.

3. To make the sauce, let the pan cool down a little, then add the oil. Tip in the onion and garlic and fry for 2–3 minutes over medium heat. Add the passata, tomato paste and sugar, cover with a lid, bring to a simmer and cook for 10 minutes.

4. Add the browned meatballs back into the pan, cover again and simmer for a further 10 minutes until the meatballs are completely cooked through.

5. Meanwhile, cook the spaghetti in plenty of boiling salted water according to the packet instructions, then drain.

6. Serve five meatballs per person on a pile of spaghetti and with some of the remaining Parmesan sprinkled on top.

Mary's Classic Tips:
* To brown the meatballs evenly, place them in the frying pan as if around a clock face. Sit the first at '12 o'clock' and place the next ones in a clockwise direction. When they have cooked for 3–4 minutes and need turning, start from the first meatball and move around the pan in sequence, turning the others depending on how much time they have had cooking.
* When you turn the meatballs, be sure to do so carefully, with a gentle touch, so they do not fall apart.

Classic Lasagne

SERVES 6–8 / COOK TIME: 1½ hours

8 sheets of dried (no pre-
cook) lasagne
1 x 125g ball of mozzarella,
drained and chopped
75g (3oz) mature Cheddar
cheese, grated

For the meat sauce
1 tbsp olive oil
2 onions, chopped
800g (1¾lb) lean minced beef
2 garlic cloves, crushed
3 tbsp tomato purée
200ml (7fl oz) red wine
2 x 400g tins of chopped
tomatoes
A few drops of
Worcestershire sauce
A pinch of sugar
1 large bunch of basil,
chopped
Salt and freshly ground
black pepper

For the white sauce
50g (2oz) butter
50g (2oz) plain flour
600ml (1 pint) hot milk
2 tsp Dijon mustard
50g (2oz) Parmesan cheese,
grated

An Italian classic, but now a classic here too! Using dried lasagne sheets, I like to leave the assembled lasagne for about 2 hours to soften before cooking. This is rich tasting and delicious and it's very cheesy with a deep rich, tomatoey sauce. The mozzarella adds a lovely stringy texture.

1. You will need a 2.3–3-litre (4–5-pint) square or rectangular ovenproof dish (see tip). Preheat the oven to 200°C/ 180°C fan/Gas 6.

2. First make the meat sauce. Heat the oil in a large frying pan, add the onions and fry over a medium heat for 2–3 minutes. Add the beef and brown over a high heat for 2–3 minutes, breaking the mince up with a wooden spoon or spatula. Add the garlic and tomato purée and cook for 30 seconds.

3. Pour in the red wine, chopped tomatoes and Worcestershire sauce and add the sugar. Cover with a lid and simmer over a low heat for about 45 minutes until tender. Season with salt and pepper and stir in the basil.

4. Shortly before the meat sauce is ready, make the white sauce. Melt the butter in a saucepan. Add the flour and stir over the heat for 30 seconds. Gradually stir in the hot milk, whisking, until you have a thickened, smooth sauce. Add the mustard and cheese and season to taste with salt and pepper.

....

5. To assemble the lasagne, spread a third of the meat sauce over the base of the ovenproof dish. Blob over a third of the white sauce and arrange four sheets of lasagne in a single layer on top. Spoon over another third each of the meat sauce and the white sauce, sprinkle over the mozzarella and then arrange another four lasagne sheets over the top. Spoon over the remaining meat sauce and white sauce and sprinkle with the Cheddar cheese.

6. Place on a baking tray, if necessary, to catch any drips, and bake in the oven for 35–40 minutes until golden and bubbling.

Step-by-step images overleaf →

Mary's Classic Tip:
* A rectangular dish is best suited to the rectangular shape of the lasagne sheets, helping to avoid too much overlap between the sheets. Break up the sheets, otherwise, to ensure they fit in an even layer and cover well with the sauce so that the edges don't burn during cooking.
* If cooking the lasagne straight away, it is best to soak the sheets of lasagne in hot water for 10 minutes before assembling. This makes sure they will be soft and cooked.

Making the Classic Lasagne:

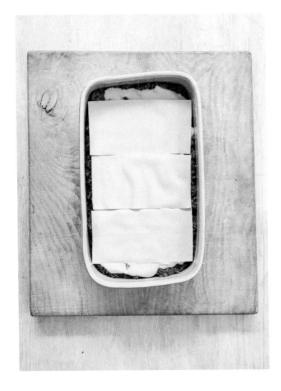

Prime Roast Rib of Beef

SERVES 6–8 / COOK TIME: 2 hours, plus resting

1 x 2-rib joint of beef,
  either prime rib or wing
  rib (about 2.7kg/6lb)
Oil, for rubbing into the beef
Mustard powder,
  for sprinkling
2 onions, peeled and cut
  in half
1 celery stick, chopped into
  6 pieces

For the gravy
2 tbsp plain flour
150ml (5fl oz) red wine
300ml (10fl oz) beef stock
  (optional)
1 tsp Worcestershire sauce
A few drops of gravy
  browning

Prepare Ahead:
Any leftovers can be eaten
cold the next day.

Rib of beef is a particularly tasty joint because of the fat marbling throughout. It looks impressive and tastes tender and succulent. Wing rib beef comes from the sirloin end and is a little more expensive.

1. Preheat the oven to the 240°C/220°C fan/Gas 9.

2. Rub some oil over the beef and sprinkle with a little mustard powder. Arrange the onion halves and celery pieces in a large roasting tin and sit the beef on top.

3. Transfer to the oven and roast for 20 minutes. Turn the temperature down to 200°C/180°C fan/Gas 6 and roast for a further 15 minutes per 450g (1lb) (see tip).

4. Remove the beef from the tin and leave to rest for a minimum of 20 minutes before carving, wrapped in foil to keep warm.

5. Meanwhile, make the gravy. Remove the onion and celery from the roasting tin and pour off most of the fat (see tip), leaving a couple of tablespoons in the tin. Stir in the flour and cook over a medium heat for a minute, stirring in all the sediment from the tin to boost the flavour. Add the wine and boil for a few minutes, then gradually stir in the stock (or the water from cooking any vegetables), along with some of the meat juices, and bring back up to the boil. Simmer for a few minutes and add the Worcestershire sauce and gravy browning (if using).

6. Serve the beef with Yorkshire puddings, roast potatoes or Parisienne Potatoes (see page 174) and vegetables such as carrots and broccoli. Don't forget the horseradish sauce!

Continued overleaf →

Using a Meat Thermometer: Ovens vary a lot in how efficient they are, and thermostats are not always accurate. The shape and size of a joint of meat makes a difference too: a thicker piece weighing the same amount as a longer, thinner joint will take a bit longer to roast, for instance. This is where a meat thermometer can come in very handy, ensuring that the meat is cooked to your liking; just make sure the thermometer is not touching a bone when testing. Beef is rare at an internal temperature of 60°C/140°F, medium at 70°C/160°F and well done at 75°C/165°F – this is the thermometer reading when the joint comes out of the oven, and allows time for resting, during which time the internal temperature of the meat will continue to rise by as much as 10°C.

Mary's Classic Tips:

* This is for rare beef; cook for a further 20 or 25 minutes per 450g (1lb) if you prefer your meat medium or well done, bearing in mind that the internal temperature of the meat continues to rise after resting (see 'Using a Meat Thermometer' above).
* Make sure you save all the dripping from the joint; it's perfect for roasting potatoes or for cooking Yorkshire puddings and will keep in the fridge until the following week.

Beef Bourguignon

SERVES 6 / COOK TIME: 2½ hours

2 tbsp sunflower oil
1kg (2lb 3oz) braising beef, diced
250g (9oz) rashers of smoked back bacon, diced
500g (1lb 2oz) shallots, peeled
2 celery sticks, sliced
2 large garlic cloves, crushed
2 tbsp tomato purée
50g (2oz) plain flour
450ml (15fl oz) red wine
150ml (5fl oz) beef stock
1 tbsp muscovado sugar
5 bay leaves
500g (1lb 2oz) button mushrooms

Prepare Ahead:
Can be made up to 3 days ahead. Add the mushrooms when reheating to serve.

Freeze:
Freezes well.

A true favourite when cooking for friends when the nights draw in. It can easily be made ahead.

1. Preheat the oven to 160°C/140°C fan/Gas 3.

2. Heat the oil in a deep ovenproof frying pan with a lid or a flameproof and ovenproof casserole dish. Add half the beef and brown over a high heat for 4–5 minutes until golden and sealed. Remove from the pan with a slotted spoon and set aside on a plate before browning the remaining beef in the same way (see tip). Add the bacon to the pan and fry for 3–4 minutes until crisp, then set aside with the beef.

3. Place the shallots and celery in the pan and fry for 3–4 minutes until lightly golden, then add the garlic and tomato purée and cook for 30 seconds. Whisk the flour with a little of the wine in a bowl to make a smooth paste, add the remaining wine and whisk until smooth (see tip).

4. Add the wine mixture to the pan with the stock, sugar and bay leaves and stir until thickened. Add the browned beef and bacon and bring to the boil, then cover with a lid and transfer to the oven to cook for about 2 hours or until tender. Check halfway through cooking and add some extra stock or hot water, if needed.

5. Add the mushrooms and simmer for another 10 minutes. Season well with salt and pepper and remove the bay leaves. Serve piping hot with mash and a green vegetable.

Mary's Classic Tips:
* The beef is browned in two batches so as not to overcrowd the pan. Less meat in the pan keeps the temperature nice and hot, ensuring that the beef browns well.
* It's important to get the wine and flour paste smooth and lump-free before it is added to the pan, as once it's mixed in with the stock, it's much harder to beat out any gloopy lumps of flour.

VEGETARIAN

·

SALADS

·

SIDE DISHES

Pistou Linguine

SERVES 4–6 as a main dish / COOK TIME: 10 minutes

300g (11oz) linguine pasta
25g (1oz) butter
500g (1lb 2oz) chestnut
  mushrooms, sliced
75g (3oz) Parmesan cheese,
  grated

For the pistou sauce
4 tbsp roughly chopped
  flat-leaf parsley
4 tbsp roughly chopped basil
2 tbsp roughly
  snipped chives
2 garlic cloves, crushed
Juice of 1 lemon (see tip)
200g (7oz) full-fat
  crème fraîche
Salt and freshly ground
  black pepper

Prepare Ahead:
The pistou sauce can be
made up to a day ahead
and kept in the fridge.

Pistou is a classic Provençal sauce made of basil, garlic and oil, similar to pesto but without the pine nuts and Parmesan.

1. To make the pistou sauce, place the herbs, garlic, lemon juice and crème fraîche in a food processor and whizz until the herbs are finely chopped. Season well with salt and pepper.

2. Cook the linguine in boiling salted water according to the packet instructions, then drain, reserving 2 tablespoons of the pasta cooking water (see tip).

3. While the pasta is cooking, melt the butter in a deep frying pan, add the mushrooms and fry over a high heat for about 1–2 minutes. Cover with a lid and cook over a low heat for 3 minutes, then remove the lid and fry over a high heat until golden and all the liquid has evaporated. Spoon the mushrooms into a bowl.

4. Add the pistou sauce and the reserved pasta water to the frying pan and heat until just boiling. Tip in the cooked pasta, season with salt and pepper and toss until coated and warmed through. Remove from the heat, add most of the Parmesan and mushrooms and toss to combine.

5. Tip into a bowl, scatter with the remaining Parmesan and mushrooms and taste for seasoning.

Mary's Classic Tips:
* Roll the lemon on a board before squeezing to get the most juice from it.
* The Parmesan really thickens the sauce so it coats the pasta. For a thinner sauce, reserve some extra pasta water and add more than 2 tablespoons in step 4.

Vegetable Tortilla

SERVES 2 / COOK TIME: 35–45 minutes

3 tbsp olive oil
1 onion, thinly sliced
½ red pepper, deseeded
   and diced
225g (8oz) potatoes, peeled
   and cut into slices about
   1cm (½in) thick
4 large eggs
1 tbsp finely chopped parsley
Salt and freshly ground
   black pepper

Prepare Ahead:
While the tortilla is best
served immediately, you can
leave it to cool and serve
cold, cut into wedges –
perfect for picnics or
lunchboxes. Best eaten on
the same day.

Mary's Classic Tip:
* The secret to success is to
   be sure that the base of the
   tortilla moves freely before
   turning it over. The egg
   needs to set around the
   potato to hold it all
   together, otherwise it will
   stick to the pan and fall
   apart once turned.

Layers of potato, onion and peppers in an omelette, cooked on the hob; a delicious brunch, lunch or light supper. A frittata is similar but half cooked in the oven.

1. You will need a small heavy-based frying pan, preferably non-stick, about 20cm (8in) in diameter and with a lid.

2. Heat 2 tablespoons of the oil in the pan, add the onion and fry over a medium-high heat for 5 minutes. Add the pepper and potatoes, mix with the onions so all the vegetables are well coated in the oil, and season with salt and pepper. Cover with the lid and gently cook over a low heat for about 15–20 minutes until the potatoes are cooked through.

3. Meanwhile, beat the eggs in a bowl, seasoning with salt and pepper. When the vegetables are done, add them to the eggs and mix together.

4. Wipe the pan clean and add the remaining oil, then carefully pour in the egg mixture and sprinkle with parsley. Heat until the sides and top of the tortilla have just set and the base is lightly golden brown. This takes around 10–15 minutes.

5. When the middle is almost set, with just a little wobble, and the base moves freely away from the pan (see tip), carefully slide on to a plate. You may need a flexible spatula to help you here. Put the pan on top and flip over to cook the other side for about 3–4 minutes until golden all over and just cooked through.

6. Slide on to a plate to serve. You may want to put a plate on top of the pan (taking care as it's hot) and flip the tortilla on to it so that the side with the parsley is on top.

Step-by-step images overleaf →

Making the Vegetable Tortilla:

Squash, Brie & Cranberry Tarts

MAKES **12 tarts** / COOK TIME: 40–50 minutes, plus resting

500g (1lb 2oz) peeled
   butternut squash, diced
   into 1cm (½in) cubes
1 large onion, chopped
2 tbsp olive oil
4–5 sheets of filo pastry
50g (2oz) butter, melted,
   plus extra for greasing
3 tsp cranberry sauce
   (from a jar)
2 eggs
250ml (9fl oz) double cream
225g (8oz) just-ripe Brie,
   chilled until firm
Paprika, for sprinkling
Salt and freshly ground
   black pepper

Prepare Ahead:

Can be made up to a day
ahead and reheated on a
baking sheet in a hot oven
for 10 minutes to crisp up
the pastry.

Freeze:

The cooked tarts freeze well
cooked. Pack them carefully
in a freezer box as the filo
pastry case is very delicate
once cooked.

**Full of flavour and perfect for a starter, light lunch or picnic.
A lovely recipe, delicious and a bit different.**

1. You will need a 12-hole muffin tin. Preheat the oven to
   200°C/180°C fan/Gas 6 and grease the muffin tin with butter.

2. Scatter the butternut squash and onion in a large roasting
   tin, drizzle over the oil, season with salt and pepper and toss
   together. Roast in the oven for 20–25 minutes until tender
   and lightly golden. Set aside to cool.

3. Lay the sheets of filo pastry on a worktop and brush with
   melted butter (see tip). Cut out 24 x 12cm (5in) squares of filo.
   Put one square on a board and place another square on top
   at an angle to give a star shape. Carefully lift the filo star and
   place in a mould of the muffin tin. Gently press it down, letting
   the tips of the pastry stick up above the tin. Continue with the
   remaining squares, filling the moulds of the tin until it is full.

4. Divide the cold squash and onion mixture among the pastry
   cases. Top each with a ¼ teaspoon of the cranberry sauce. Break
   the eggs into a jug, add the cream, season with salt and pepper
   and whisk until smooth. Pour the custard over the filling, making
   sure it doesn't overflow the edges of the pastry case.

5. Cut the Brie into 24 thin slices, trimming the lengths if too
   long, and top each tart with a cross of Brie. Sprinkle lightly
   with paprika.

6. Bake for 20–25 minutes until golden and the pastry is crisp
   underneath. Leave to settle in the tin for 10–15 minutes until
   the filling sets, then remove each tart with a palette knife or
   table knife, taking care not to break the cases. Serve warm.

Mary's Classic Tip:
* Filo pastry is easy to work with when it is fresh, but it dries
   out quickly and becomes more fragile. Keep any unused pastry
   under a clean damp tea towel to stop it becoming brittle.

Leek & Stilton Tart

SERVES 6–8 as a light meal / CHILLING TIME: 15 minutes / COOK TIME: 1½ hours, plus resting

For the shortcrust pastry
225g (8oz) plain flour, plus
    extra for dusting
125g (4½oz) cold butter,
    cubed, plus extra
    for greasing
1 egg, beaten with
    1 tbsp water

For the filling
1 tbsp olive oil
2 leeks, thinly sliced
2 celery sticks, thinly sliced
4 eggs
450ml (15fl oz) double cream
150g (5oz) Stilton cheese,
    coarsely grated
2 tbsp chopped parsley
Salt and freshly ground
    black pepper

Quiche, tart, all the same and all with a thin layer of pastry and an abundant filling. Although it looks a long cooking time, this can be prepared in easy stages: cooking the base first and leaving to cool, and then filling later.

1. You will need a 28cm (11in) round, loose-bottomed deep tart tin, preferably fluted. Preheat the oven to 200°C/180°C fan/Gas 6 and grease the tin with butter.

2. To make the pastry, measure the flour and butter into a food processor and whizz until the mixture resembles breadcrumbs. Add the beaten egg and water and whizz into a smooth ball of dough. Alternatively, rub the flour and butter together in a mixing bowl with your fingertips before adding the egg and water.

3. Roll the pastry out on a lightly floured work surface to a disc slightly larger than the tin and about the thickness of a £1 coin. Carefully transfer the pastry to the tin and press it into the base and sides. Form a little lip around the edges of the tin, trim off any excess and prick the base with a fork. Place in the fridge to chill for about 15 minutes.

4. Line the pastry case with baking paper and baking beans and bake blind in the oven for 15 minutes. Remove the beans and paper and return to the oven for a further 5–10 minutes or until just cooked and pale golden. Reduce the oven temperature to 180°C/160°C fan/Gas 4.

Continued overleaf →

5. Meanwhile, make the filling. Heat the oil in a wide-based frying pan, add the leeks and celery and fry over a high heat for 2–3 minutes. Reduce the heat to low, cover with a lid and simmer for 20–25 minutes or until the vegetables are completely tender. Take off the lid, then increase the heat and fry for another minute to drive off any excess liquid. Remove the pan from the heat.

6. Beat the eggs and cream together in a jug and season with salt and pepper.

7. Spoon the cooked leeks and celery into the pastry case, scatter with the cheese and parsley and season with salt and pepper. Pour over the egg and cream mixture.

8. Bake in the oven for about 35–40 minutes or until golden brown and just set on top (see tip). Leave for 5–10 minutes to rest before turning out.

Prepare Ahead:
Can be made up to 8 hours ahead and reheated. The pastry base can be cooked up to a day ahead.

Freeze:
Both the cooked tart and the unfilled pastry base freeze well.

Mary's Classic Tip:
* Check the tart halfway through cooking and if it is browning on one side more than the other, turn it around on the oven shelf.

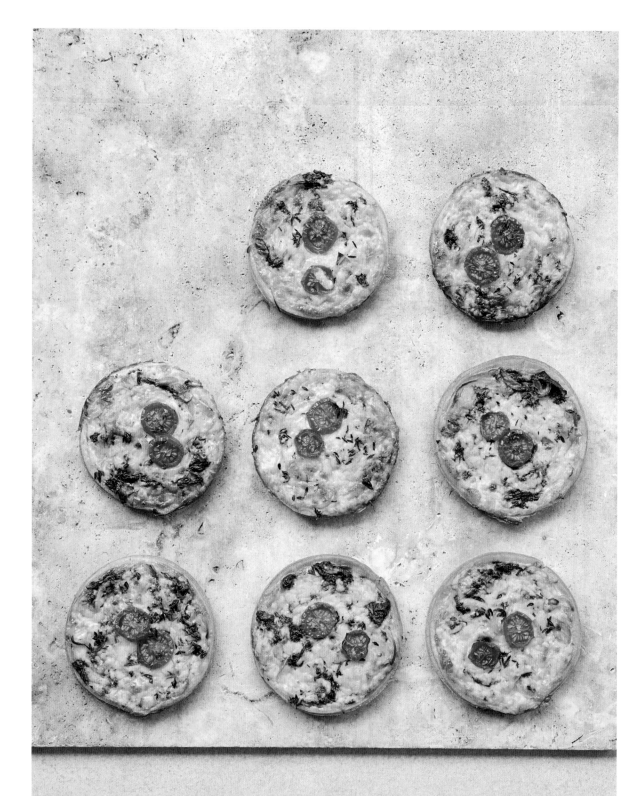

Individual Cheese, Tomato & Thyme Tartlets

MAKES **8 tartlets** / CHILLING TIME: **30 minutes** / COOK TIME: **30–40 minutes**

For the pastry
175g (6oz) plain flour, plus
    extra for dusting
1 tsp mustard powder
75g (3oz) cold butter, cut
    into small pieces, plus
    extra for greasing
50g (2oz) Parmesan cheese,
    finely grated
1 large egg, beaten

For the filling
1 tbsp olive oil
1 large onion, thinly sliced
200g (7oz) baby spinach
100g (4oz) mature Cheddar
    cheese, grated
2 large eggs
300ml (10fl oz) double cream
8 cherry tomatoes, sliced
    (see tip)
1 tbsp chopped fresh thyme
    leaves (see tip)
Salt and freshly ground
    black pepper

Perfect for a starter, light lunch or picnic. Shallow, colourful, rich and full of flavour.

1. You will need two 4-hole Yorkshire pudding tins, with moulds about 10cm (4in) in diameter and 2cm (¾in) deep, and a 11.5cm (4½in) plain pastry cutter. Lightly grease the Yorkshire pudding tins with butter.

2. First make the pastry. Measure the flour, mustard powder and butter into a food processor and whizz until the mixture resembles fine breadcrumbs. Add the cheese and the beaten egg and mix again, for just as long as it takes for the ingredients to come together. Alternatively, rub the flour, mustard powder and butter together in a mixing bowl with your fingertips before adding the cheese and beaten egg.

3. Roll the pastry to the thickness of a £1 coin on a lightly floured work surface and use the pastry cutter to stamp out eight discs a little larger than the moulds, re-rolling the pastry as needed. The pastry needs to be above the edge. Use the discs to line the prepared Yorkshire pudding moulds. Prick the bases with a fork and then place in the fridge to chill for 30 minutes while you make the filling.

4. Preheat the oven to 200°C/180°C fan/Gas 6 and put two heavy baking sheets in the oven to get hot.

5. Heat the oil in a pan and cook the onion over a high heat for 2–3 minutes. Lower the heat, cover with a lid and cook for about 15 minutes or until soft and lightly golden.

Continued overleaf →

6. Meanwhile, put the kettle on to boil. Sit the spinach in a colander in the sink and pour over the boiling water to wilt the leaves. Refresh in cold water to keep the colour, then press with the back of a spoon to squeeze out as much of the water as possible. Tip the drained spinach on to a board and coarsely chop. Return the onion to a high heat to fry for a minute to drive off any excess moisture, add the spinach and stir for a minute. Remove from the heat and set aside to cool.

7. Divide the cooled onion and spinach among the tartlet cases and top with the cheese. Beat the eggs together in a jug, add the double cream and season with salt and pepper. Carefully pour some of the egg and cream mixture into each of the tartlets and place two tomato slices on top. Sprinkle the thyme leaves over the middle.

8. Bake in the oven on the hot baking sheets for 15–20 minutes until set and pale golden. Turn the tins around halfway through the cooking time, swapping them between the oven shelves if necessary to ensure they cook evenly. Serve warm.

Prepare Ahead:
Can be made up to a day ahead and reheated to serve.

Freeze:
The tartlets freeze well.

Mary's Classic Tips:
* Use a serrated knife to cut these small tomatoes without squashing them.
* Do not be tempted to use dried thyme – only fresh will do.

Vegetable Stir-Fry

SERVES 6 as a main dish / COOK TIME: 7–8 minutes

100g (4oz) medium
   egg noodles
2 tbsp sunflower oil
1 large onion, sliced
2 carrots, peeled and cut
   into thin matchsticks
2 red peppers, deseeded
   and cut into 4cm
   (1½in) pieces
200g (7oz) button
   mushrooms, halved
200g (7oz) broccoli, cut into
   small florets (see tip)
½ head Chinese cabbage,
   sliced (white and green
   parts separated)
1 small bunch of coriander,
   chopped
Salt and freshly ground
   black pepper

For the sauce
3 tbsp hoisin sauce
3 tbsp soy sauce, plus extra
   to serve
2 tbsp sweet chilli sauce,
   plus extra to serve
1 garlic clove, crushed

Fresh, crunchy and full of flavour – perfect for a fast but healthy midweek meal.

1. Cook the noodles in a saucepan of boiling water according to the packet instructions.

2. Meanwhile, mix all of the sauce ingredients together in a small bowl.

3. Heat the sunflower oil in a large frying pan or wok. Add the onion, carrots and red peppers and stir-fry over a high heat for 2 minutes. Stir in the mushrooms and broccoli, cover with a tight-fitting lid and steam for 3–4 minutes, still over a high heat and shaking the pan from time to time.

4. Remove the lid and add the white parts of the Chinese cabbage and the sauce. Toss over the heat for a minute or so to combine, and season with pepper and a little salt.

5. Drain the noodles and add to the pan with the coriander and green parts of the Chinese cabbage. Toss together and serve at once, otherwise the Chinese cabbage goes limp (see tip). Season with extra soy sauce and sweet chilli sauce.

Mary's Classic Tips:
* The broccoli needs to be cut into small florets, and a similar size to the other vegetables, so that it cooks in just 3–4 minutes.
* You could add some toasted cashew nuts for extra protein and crunch, if you like.

Wild Mushroom Galettes

SERVES 6 as a starter or light meal / CHILLING TIME: 10 minutes / COOK TIME: 25–30 minutes

1 x 500g block of all-butter
    puff pastry
Plain flour, for dusting
1 egg, beaten

For the mushroom filling
3 tbsp sunflower oil
A knob of butter
1–2 large garlic cloves,
    crushed
250g (9oz) chestnut
    mushrooms, quartered
    (see tip)
250g (9oz) large flat
    mushrooms, sliced into
    8 wedges
250g (9oz) mixed wild
    mushrooms (such as oyster
    and shiitake), thickly sliced
400g (14oz) full-fat crème
    fraîche
50g (2oz) Parmesan cheese,
    grated
Juice of ½ lemon
Salt and freshly ground
    black pepper
2 tbsp chopped parsley,
    to garnish

These are a wonderful first course or light lunch. Classic garlic mushrooms in a delicious creamy sauce filling a flaky puff pastry galette. A modern twist on the old-fashioned vol-au-vent and much easier to make.

1. You will need an 8.5cm (3½in) plain pastry cutter. Preheat the oven to 200°C/180°C fan/Gas 6 and line a baking sheet with baking paper.

2. Roll out the pastry on a floured work surface into a rectangle measuring 20 x 28cm (8 x 11in) and 7–8mm (⅓in) thick.

3. Lightly score a criss-cross pattern over the surface of the pastry, making sure not to cut all the way through. Use the pastry cutter to stamp out six discs, taking care not to twist the cutter in the pastry, to ensure the discs rise evenly.

4. Place on the lined baking sheet, spaced well apart, and chill in the fridge for about 10 minutes. Brush the tops of the discs with the beaten egg.

5. Meanwhile, place the largest roasting tin that you have in the oven to heat up for a few minutes until hot. Add the sunflower oil, butter, garlic and all the mushrooms (see tip). Season with salt and pepper and toss together.

6. Put the roasting tin on a shelf near the bottom of the oven and place the baking sheet with the pastry on a shelf near the top. Bake for about 18–20 minutes or until the galettes are well risen and lightly golden. The mushrooms should be brown and most of the juices should have evaporated from the tin.

Continued overleaf →

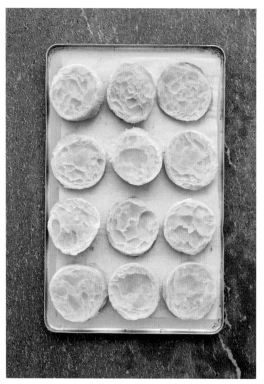

7. Remove both trays from the oven. Carefully slice the galettes in half horizontally and remove any uncooked pastry from the very middle of each galette so the sides form a cup. Place upside down on the baking sheet.

8. Add the crème fraîche to the roasting tin and mix in. Put both trays back into the oven to cook for another 8–10 minutes or until the pastry cases are crisp. The mushrooms should be softened and the crème fraîche will have formed a mushroom-coloured sauce.

9. Add the Parmesan and lemon juice to the tin, stirring to melt the cheese, then season to taste with salt and pepper.

10. Spoon the mushroom mixture into one half of each of the pastry cases. Garnish with the chopped parsley and top with the remaining half.

Prepare Ahead:
The galettes can be made a day in advanced and stored in an airtight container.

Mary's Classic Tips:
* Try not to wash mushrooms; just give them a wipe with kitchen paper or use a small brush to remove any dirt.
* Any small and delicate wild mushrooms should be added with the crème fraîche in step 8.

Waldorf Salad

SERVES 6–8 as a light meal / COOK TIME: 3–4 minutes

100g (4oz) walnut pieces
2 Ruby Gem lettuces
   (see tip), sliced
1 x 85g bag of mixed
   salad leaves
2 celery hearts, sliced
1 Granny Smith apple,
   cored and thinly sliced
150g (5oz) seedless green
   grapes, halved

For the blue cheese dressing
100g (4oz) Roquefort cheese,
   roughly cubed
Juice of 1 small lemon
150ml (5fl oz) soured cream
1 tsp sugar
Salt and freshly ground
   black pepper

Prepare Ahead:
The dressing can be made up
to 2 days ahead. The salad
can be assembled up to
2 hours ahead, adding the
sliced apple and dressing
to serve.

A wonderful classic, crunchy salad. If you cannot get Roquefort cheese, use Stilton instead.

1. Place the walnuts in a small frying pan and toast over a medium heat, tossing frequently, for 3–4 minutes or until starting to brown, then set aside to cool.

2. Arrange the lettuce leaves in a large salad bowl with the celery, apple, grapes and toasted walnuts.

3. Measure all the ingredients for the dressing into a small free-standing blender or food processor. Whizz together until smooth and season to taste with salt and pepper.

4. Drizzle the dressing over the salad, toss together and serve at once (see tip).

Mary's Classic Tips:
* If you can't find Ruby Gem lettuces, use standard Little Gems instead – the mixed salad leaves will help provide the extra colour.
* For non-vegetarians, a handful of crispy bacon pieces scattered over the top goes extremely well with this dish.

Roast Garlic Potatoes

SERVES 6 as a side dish / COOK TIME: 40–45 minutes

1.2kg (2lb 10oz) floury
   potatoes (such as Maris
   Piper), peeled and cut into
   2.5cm (1in) dice
2 tbsp sunflower oil
50g (2oz) butter, softened
2–3 garlic cloves, crushed
Salt

Golden brown and feeling very French, the family love these crispy cubes of potato. We eat them with Cannon of Lamb with Minted Spring Vegetables (page 129) and they are delicious.

1. Preheat the oven 220°C/200°C fan/Gas 7 and leave a large roasting tin in the oven for a few minutes to get very hot.

2. Meanwhile, add the potato cubes to a large saucepan of salted water and bring to the boil. Boil for about 3 minutes, then drain the potatoes and return to the pan. Cover with a lid, give the potatoes a shake and leave to steam for a few minutes.

3. Add the sunflower oil to the pan and carefully toss the potatoes so that they are coated in the oil. Tip into the hot roasting tin and roast in the oven for about 20–25 minutes, turning over halfway through.

4. Add the butter and garlic to a bowl and mash together using a fork. Blob the garlic butter over the potatoes (see tip), season with salt and return to the oven to cook for about 10 minutes or until golden and crisp.

Mary's Classic Tip:
* Adding the garlic butter to the potatoes in the final cooking
   stage ensures the crushed garlic doesn't burn in the hot oven.

Parisienne Potatoes

SERVES 6 as a side dish / COOK TIME: 30–35 minutes

Butter, for greasing
1.5kg (3lb) floury potatoes
   (such as Maris Piper),
   peeled
1 large onion, sliced into
   14–16 wedges
300ml (10fl oz) double cream
75g (3oz) Gruyère cheese
   (see tip), grated
Salt and freshly ground
   black pepper

....

Prepare Ahead:
Can be assembled up to
12 hours ahead.

So often when raw potatoes, onion and cream are cooked the natural juices curdle the cream. Here I have boiled the potatoes and onions for a short time so you will not have that problem. Very rich and delicious, this method definitely solves the problem of curdling.

1. You will need a 3-litre (5-pint) shallow ovenproof dish. Preheat the oven to 220°C/200°C fan/Gas 7 and grease the dish with butter.

2. Cut the potatoes into 2cm (¾in) cubes or thick slices and place in a large saucepan. Add the onion and cover with cold salted water. Bring to the boil and boil for about 10 minutes or until the potatoes are just cooked.

3. Drain in a colander and then tip the potatoes and onion wedges into the prepared ovenproof dish, season with salt and pepper and pour over the cream. Sprinkle with the cheese and cook in the oven for 15–20 minutes or until golden brown and bubbling.

Mary's Classic Tip:
* Gruyère cheese gives a wonderful deep flavour. Use Cheddar if preferred.

Masses of Mash

SERVES 6 as a side dish / COOK TIME: 15–20 minutes

1kg (2lb 3oz) Maris Piper or
   King Edward potatoes
A splash of milk
A knob of butter
Salt and freshly ground
   black pepper

Prepare Ahead:
Can be made up to
6 hours ahead.

Potato must be one of our nation's favourite vegetables, and mash is such a versatile way to serve it with many dishes. Choose a starchy, fluffy, not too waxy potato.

1. Peel the potatoes and cut into even-sized cubes. Place in a pan of cold, salted water and bring to the boil. Cook for 15–20 minutes or until tender, and you are able to slip a knife into them easily.

2. Drain, add the milk and butter, season with salt and pepper and mash until smooth, then beat with a hand whisk or wooden spoon until smooth and creamy (see tip).

3. Serve the mash as it is or choose one of the options below to make it extra special!

Mash Options:

Unless otherwise indicated, all the following go with either meat or fish and should be stirred into the basic mash.

Mustard Mash (pictured opposite, top left): About 2 tablespoons of grainy mustard and 1 rounded tablespoon of Dijon mustard.

Leek Mash: 1 good-sized leek, sliced into rings, boiled with the potatoes and mashed together.

Horseradish Mash: About 5 tablespoons of hot creamed horseradish (just 2 tablespoons for the hot variety). Taste as you go – add more for a stronger hit! This mash goes well with meat, especially beef.

Spring Onion and Soured Cream Mash: (pictured opposite, top right): 1 small bunch of spring onions (3–4), finely sliced and stirred through the mash with 2 good tablespoons of soured cream instead of the milk.

Continued overleaf →

Fresh Herb Mash (pictured page 176, bottom left): 2 tablespoons each of finely chopped parsley, chives and thyme leaves.

Caper and Dill Mash: 2 tablespoons of rinsed and chopped capers and 2 tablespoons of chopped dill. This goes well with fish.

Cheesy Mash: About 75g (3oz) mature Cheddar cheese, coarsely grated and stirred in well so that it melts into the mash.

Olive Oil Mash: Replace the butter and milk with 2 tablespoons of good olive oil. Add a few shavings of truffle over the top for a posh touch *(pictured page 176, bottom right).*

Fried Onion Mash: Fry very thin slices of one white onion in olive oil over high heat until and golden and crispy. Sprinkle over the mash to serve.

Potato and Celeriac Mash: Replace half the potatoes with celeriac, peeled and cubed, and cook both together as in the main recipe on page 177. Add 100ml (3½fl oz) full-fat crème fraîche instead of the milk and butter.

Potato and Swede Mash: Replace half the potatoes with swede, peeled and cubed, and cook both together as in the main recipe on page 177. Add some coarsely ground black pepper and a generous amount of butter to the mash.

Mary's Classic Tip:
* Use an electric whisk and don't overbeat or the mash will be gloopy.

Baked Fennel Gratin with Mascarpone

SERVES 6 as a side dish / COOK TIME: 20–25 minutes

600g (1lb 5oz) fennel bulbs
  (about 2 large bulbs)
2 garlic cloves, crushed
250g (9oz) full-fat
  mascarpone cheese
50g (2oz) Cheddar cheese,
  grated
25g (1oz) Gruyère cheese,
  grated
Paprika, for sprinkling
Salt and freshly ground
  black pepper

Prepare Ahead:
Can be assembled up
to 8 hours ahead.

This is delicious! Hearty and comforting – similar to a potato dauphinoise but without the carbs and the lengthy prep. We serve it with Beef Bourguignon (page 149), or it would be nice with a roast dinner too.

1. Preheat the oven to 220°C/200°C fan/Gas 7.

2. Cut the fennel in half lengthways through the root and then lengthways into slices about 1cm (½in) thick, removing the woody root. Cook in a saucepan of boiling salted water for about 8 minutes or until just tender, then drain in a colander and dry well (see tip).

3. Arrange in a shallow ovenproof dish and season with salt and black pepper.

4. Mix the garlic and mascarpone together in a bowl and blob spoonfuls over the fennel. Scatter with the grated cheeses and sprinkle with a light dusting of paprika.

5. Bake in the oven for about 15–20 minutes or until bubbling and lightly golden.

Mary's Classic Tip:
* It's important to dry the fennel well after it has been boiled, so no excess water is added to the creamy mascarpone sauce as it cooks. Gently pat the fennel dry with kitchen paper while it is in the colander, taking care as the cooked slices are now tender and you want them to keep their shape.

Corn on the Cob with Chilli Herb Butter

SERVES 6 as side dish / CHILLING TIME: A minimum of 30 minutes / COOK TIME: 5–10 minutes

3 corn on the cob

For the chilli herb butter
50g (2oz) butter, softened
½ fresh red chilli, deseeded
   and finely chopped
1 tbsp chopped parsley
1 tbsp snipped chives
Salt and freshly ground
   black pepper

Prepare Ahead:
The corn can be cooked up
to 8 hours ahead and
reheated to serve. The chilli
herb butter can be kept in
the fridge for 3–4 days.

Freeze:
The butter freezes well.

Not something I do often, but when the grandchildren are around they love it. Both colourful and tasty.

1. Place all the ingredients for the chilli herb butter in a bowl. Season with salt and pepper and mash together. Sit the butter on a piece of cling film and then roll the cling film around the butter in a sausage shape. Seal the ends and chill in the fridge for at least 30 minutes or until hard.

2. Slice each corn in half on the diagonal to make six pieces. Cook in a pan of boiling salted water for 5–10 minutes or until just tender.

3. Pile the corn pieces into a warmed dish. Cut discs of butter from the chilled log of butter and scatter over the hot corn to melt. Serve immediately.

Mary's Classic Tip:
* These would be perfect for a barbecue: just wrap the corn in kitchen foil with a knob of butter and cook in the hot coals.

Pan-Fried Cauliflower Steaks

SERVES 4 as a light meal / COOK TIME: 15–20 minutes

1 large cauliflower (see tip)
2 tbsp sunflower oil
A knob of butter
Ground cumin, for
    sprinkling
Salt and freshly ground
    black pepper

To serve
1–2 tbsp chopped parsley
1 quantity of Mustard Sauce
    (see page 103)

Prepare Ahead:
Can be made up to 6 hours
ahead. Reheat until piping hot
in a roasting tin in the oven.

Rather than roasting florets try roasting cauliflower steaks or slices – delicious on their own. My new favourite supper using a classic ingredient.

1. Remove any outer leaves and cut the cauliflower lengthways through the root into slices about 1.5cm (⅝in) thick. You will get about four whole slices from the middle of the cauliflower and some smaller florets from the edges.

2. Heat the oil and butter in a large frying pan. When the butter has melted, add the cauliflower pieces, season with salt and pepper and add a good sprinkling of cumin. Fry over a medium heat for about 8 minutes until tender and golden brown. You will need to do this in two batches, turning over with a fish slice or spatula halfway through (see tip).

3. Transfer to a serving platter, sprinkle with parsley and serve with the mustard sauce.

Mary's Classic Tips:
* When choosing a cauliflower, look for one with a large or wide stalk base; this will give you the best complete slices, or steaks, when it is cut.
* When cooking the cauliflower steaks, put the larger pieces in the centre of the pan and the smaller florets around the edge. The steaks will take longer to cook, while the smaller florets, which will cook more quickly and need turning sooner, can be scooped up with a spoon to turn and removed once they are browned.

Roasted Vegetables with Feta & Herbs

SERVES 6 as a main dish / COOK TIME: 30–40 minutes

1 large or 2 small aubergines,
   halved lengthways and cut
   into slices about 1.5cm
   (⅝in) thick
350g (12oz) peeled butternut
   squash, cut into 2cm
   (¾in) cubes
2 medium courgettes, halved
   lengthways and cut into
   slices about 1cm (½in) thick
2 large red peppers,
   deseeded and cut into 4cm
   (1½in) chunks
4 tbsp olive oil
Salt and freshly ground
   black pepper

For the dressing
2 tbsp balsamic vinegar
4 tbsp olive oil
1 tsp caster sugar
1 rounded tsp grainy mustard
1 banana shallot, finely diced
1 garlic clove, crushed

To serve
2 tbsp chopped mint
2 tbsp chopped basil
100g (4oz) feta cheese,
   crumbled (optional)

Roasted vegetables have become a classic over the last few decades as people see that Mediterranean vegetables are now easy to buy or grow.

1. Preheat the oven to 220°C/200°C fan/Gas 7 and line two large baking sheets with baking paper (see tip).

2. Place the vegetables in a large bowl, then add the olive oil, season with salt and pepper and toss until coated. Arrange in a single layer on the lined baking sheets.

3. Roast in the oven for 30–40 minutes until golden and a little charred, turning them halfway through if needed. The vegetables will all be cooked when the squash is tender. Leave to cool on the baking sheets.

4. Place all of the dressing ingredients in a jug, then mix well and season with salt and pepper.

5. Put the roasted vegetables on a serving platter or in a bowl, pour over the dressing and check the seasoning. Scatter with the chopped herbs and the feta (if using).

Prepare Ahead:
The vegetables and herbs can be prepared (sliced and chopped) up to 2 hours in advance. The dressing can be made up to a day ahead.

Mary's Classic Tip:
* The vegetables will fill two large baking sheets, so you will need to use two oven shelves. Make sure they are both positioned in the upper levels of the oven, so the vegetables all cook at roughly the same rate. Turn halfway if needed.

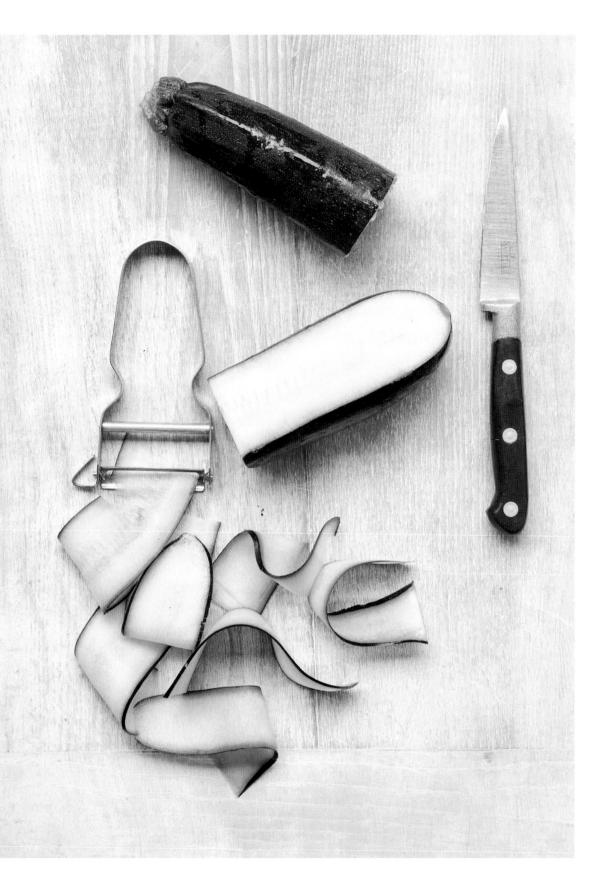

PUDDINGS

·

DESSERTS

Pears in White Wine

SERVES 6 / COOK TIME: 35 minutes, plus cooling

6 Conference pears
  (slightly under-ripe)
300ml (10fl oz) white wine
225g (8oz) caster sugar
Juice and finely grated zest
  of 1 lemon

....

Prepare Ahead:
Can be made up to 12 hours
ahead and kept in the fridge.

Such a delicious dessert and a change from fruit salad – quite spoiling. A great recipe to use up under-ripe pears.

1. Peel the pears neatly, leaving the stalks on.

2. Measure the wine and sugar into a saucepan large enough to accommodate all the pears. Pour in 600ml (1 pint) of water and add the lemon juice and zest. Stir over a low heat until the sugar has dissolved, then bring to the boil and cook for 4–5 minutes.

3. Place the pears in the pan, cover with a lid and gently simmer for about 30 minutes until softly poached and the point of a sharp knife can be inserted easily. You may need to turn the pears over halfway through.

4. Spoon the pears into a serving dish. Once the syrup has cooled down, spoon over the pears and serve cold with cream (see tip).

Mary's Classic Tip:
* There is plenty of the syrup in the pan, so you may not wish to use it all at once. Keep it in the fridge in an airtight container for 2–3 days, and use it to pour over other soft fruits, such as strawberries or melon.

Red Frangipane Tart

SERVES 8–12 / CHILLING TIME: 20 minutes / COOK TIME: 50 minutes, plus cooling

100g (4oz) caster sugar
150g (5oz) blackberries
150g (5oz) blueberries
150g (5oz) raspberries
2 tbsp cornflour
25g (1oz) flaked almonds
25g (1oz) icing sugar, sifted

For the shortcrust pastry
225g (8oz) plain flour,
    plus extra for dusting
125g (4½oz) cold butter,
    cubed, plus extra
    for greasing
25g (1oz) icing sugar
1 egg, beaten

For the frangipane
175g (6oz) butter, softened
175g (6oz) caster sugar
4 eggs
175g (6oz) ground almonds
1 tsp almond extract

This is full of loveliness and served warm with crème fraîche, it is perfect for any season. The fruits are a rich, deep red and go well with the almond flavours. This recipe makes a generous-sized tart.

1. You will need a 28cm (11in) round, loose-bottomed, fluted tart tin with 4cm (1½in) sides. Grease the tin with butter.

2. To make the pastry, measure the flour, butter and icing sugar into a food processor and whizz until the mixture is like breadcrumbs. Alternatively, place the dry ingredients in a mixing bowl and rub in the butter with your fingertips. Add the egg and 1 generous tablespoon of water and whizz again until a ball of dough is formed.

3. Roll out on a floured work surface to the thickness of a £1 coin and slightly larger than the tin. Use the pastry to line the base and sides of the tin (see tip), then trim the edges and chill in the fridge for 20 minutes.

4. Meanwhile, preheat the oven to 200°C/180°C fan/Gas 6.

5. Prick the base of the pastry with a fork and line with baking paper and baking beans. Bake blind in the oven for 15 minutes, then remove the paper and beans and bake for another 5 minutes until golden and crisp. Remove from the oven and place on a baking sheet.

6. Meanwhile, cook the fruit. Measure the caster sugar and 2 tablespoons of water into a saucepan. Gently heat, stirring, until the sugar has dissolved. Add the blackberries and blueberries and stir over a low heat for 3–4 minutes or until the fruit is just starting to soften and release its juices. Remove from the heat and gently stir in the raspberries. Sit a sieve over a bowl and carefully spoon the fruit into the sieve to drain off the liquid, keeping the berries whole. Return the drained syrup to the pan.

Continued overleaf →

7. Place the cornflour in a small bowl and mix with 2 tablespoons of cold water, stirring until smooth. Add to the syrup in the pan, whisking over a gentle heat, then bring to the boil and cook until it has thickened enough to coat the back of a spoon. Add the softened berries and set aside to cool.

8. To make the frangipane, cream the butter and sugar until pale and fluffy in a food processor or using an electric hand whisk. Add the eggs, ground almonds and almond extract and whizz until combined.

9. Spoon the cooled berries into the cooked pastry case, then dollop the frangipane over the top, spreading it carefully over the fruit and trying not to mix the two. It will form quite a thin layer, but it rises well, and it doesn't matter if some of the fruit shows through. Level the top and scatter over the flaked almonds.

10. Slide into the hot oven and bake for 30 minutes until lightly golden and just firm in the middle. Leave to cool down slightly while you make the icing.

11. Mix the icing sugar with enough water to make a smooth, spreadable mixture, then use a teaspoon to zigzag the icing over the top of the tart. Carefully remove from the tin (see tip) and transfer to a large serving plate. Serve warm or cold.

Prepare Ahead:
Can be made up to a day ahead.

Freeze:
Freezes well.

Mary's Classic Tips:
* Use a small ball of pastry to help push the pastry into the fluted sides of the tin to give a smooth finish.
* To remove the flan from the tin without breaking the pastry, place the tin on top of a can or canister, then remove the outer ring by pushing it down. Carefully slide a palette knife underneath to remove the base of the tin and transfer the tart to the serving plate.

Treacle Tart

SERVES 6 / CHILLING TIME: 30 minutes / COOK TIME: 50–60 minutes, plus resting and cooling

500g (1lb 2oz) golden syrup
Juice and finely grated zest
　of 1 large lemon
175g (6oz) white
　breadcrumbs (made from
　a loaf a few days old)

For the shortcrust pastry
175g (6oz) plain flour, plus
　extra for dusting
75g (3oz) cold butter, cubed,
　plus extra for greasing
2 tbsp icing sugar
1 egg, beaten

Prepare Ahead:
Can be made up to a day
ahead and reheated.

Freeze:
Freezes well.

Mary's Classic Tip:
* When cooking the filled
　tart, check it isn't browning
　too quickly on one side and
　turn it round in the oven if
　it is. Similarly, if the baked
　pastry crust is browning
　too quickly before the
　filling is cooked, cover it
　with a little collar of foil
　round the edges to protect
　it from burning.

Classic for so many reasons: crisp short pastry, a filling full of flavour and warming for all the family. Keep any leftover trimmings of this lovely sweet dessert pastry to make a couple of little pastries, cutting out with pretty cutters and dusting with cinnamon, or just a couple of jam tarts.

1. You will need a 20cm (8in) round, loose-bottomed, fluted tart tin with deep sides. Grease the tin with butter.

2. To make the pastry, measure the flour, butter and icing sugar into a food processor and whizz until the mixture is like breadcrumbs. Add the egg and whizz again until a ball of dough is formed. Alternatively, place the dry ingredients in a mixing bowl and rub in the butter with your fingertips.

3. Roll out on a floured work surface to the thickness of a £1 coin and slightly larger than the tin. Use the pastry to line the base and sides of the tin, pressing the pastry well into the fluted edges, then trim off any excess pastry and chill in the fridge for 30 minutes.

4. Meanwhile, preheat the oven to 200°C/180°C fan/Gas 6.

5. Prick the base of the pastry with a fork and line with baking paper and baking beans. Bake blind in the oven for 15 minutes, then remove the paper and beans and bake for another 5 minutes until golden and crisp.

6. Reduce the oven temperature to 180°C/160°C fan/Gas 4.

7. Measure the syrup into a medium saucepan and gently warm over the heat until runny. Add the lemon juice and zest and the breadcrumbs. Mix well and leave to stand for 5 minutes.

8. Pour the filling into the tart case and level the top. Bake in the oven for 30–40 minutes until pale golden and set, but with a slight softness in the middle (see tip). Allow to cool down slightly before serving.

Lemon Meringue Pie

SERVES 6–8 / CHILLING TIME: 30 minutes / COOK TIME: 1 hour–1 hour 5 minutes, plus cooling

For the shortcrust pastry
175g (6oz) plain flour, plus
    extra for dusting
75g (3oz) cold butter, cubed,
    plus extra for greasing
2 tbsp icing sugar
1 egg, beaten

For the filling
Juice and finely grated zest of
    2 large lemons
40g (1½oz) cornflour
75g (3oz) caster sugar
4 egg yolks, beaten

For the meringue topping
4 egg whites
125g (4½oz) caster sugar
    (see tip)

The filling for lemon meringue pie is very tart, which contrasts with the firm, marshmallow-like sweet meringue. Cooking low and slow gives the meringue a velvety soft texture.

1. You will need a 23cm (9in) round, loose-bottomed, fluted tart tin with deep sides. Grease the tin with butter.

2. To make the pastry, measure the flour, butter and icing sugar into a food processor and whizz until the mixture is like breadcrumbs. Add the egg and whizz again until a ball of dough is formed. Alternatively, place the dry ingredients in a mixing bowl and rub in the butter with your fingertips.

3. Roll out on a floured work surface to the thickness of a £1 coin and slightly larger than the tin. Use the pastry to line the base and sides of the tin, pressing it well into the fluted edges, then trim off any excess and chill in the fridge for 30 minutes.

4. Meanwhile, preheat the oven to 200°C/180°C fan/Gas 6.

5. Prick the base of the pastry with a fork and line with baking paper and baking beans. Bake blind in the oven for 15 minutes, then remove the paper and beans and bake for another 5 minutes until golden and crisp.

6. Reduce the oven temperature to 150°C/130°C fan/Gas 2 and make the filling.

Prepare Ahead:
Can be made up to 8 hours
in advance and served cold.

7. Add the lemon juice and zest to a small saucepan with the cornflour and 300ml (10fl oz) of water. Whisk until smooth, then place over a medium heat and whisk until thickened. Remove from the heat, add the sugar and egg yolks (separated from the egg whites used for the meringue – see tip) and whisk again until blended together. Pour into the base of the tart and level the surface, then set aside while you make the meringue topping.

8. Whisk the egg whites in a spotlessly clean bowl with an electric hand whisk until fluffy and cloud-like. Add the caster sugar a teaspoon at a time until the mixture is stiff and glossy. Spread the meringue over the lemon filling. To stop it from sinking into the warm curd, start by putting spoonfuls of meringue around the edge, so it just touches the pastry, to make a seal. Pile the rest of the meringue into the middle and spread it out to cover the top completely, swirling the top.

9. Put back in the oven to bake for 40–45 minutes until pale golden and crisp. Leave to cool for 15–30 minutes, to allow the lemon curd to firm up, before carefully removing from the tin on to a plate. Serve either warm or cold.

Mary's Classic Tips:
* White caster sugar will give a pure white, classic meringue. Golden caster sugar will give a more toffee-like result, it depends on your preference.
* If a piece of eggshell gets into your egg whites, remove it by using the rest of the shell. It acts almost like a magnet and is easier to scoop it up than with a spoon or fingers!

Pear & Apple Strudel

SERVES 6 / COOK TIME: 30–35 minutes

About 6 sheets of filo pastry
About 50g (2oz) butter, melted,
  plus extra for greasing
About 25g (1oz) fresh white
  breadcrumbs

For the filling
1 large cooking apple,
  peeled, cored and sliced
1 large just-ripe pear, peeled,
  cored and sliced
Juice and finely grated zest
  of ½ lemon
50g (2oz) demerara sugar
1 tsp mixed spice

For the icing
175g (6oz) icing sugar, sifted
A little lemon juice

Prepare Ahead:
Can be made up to 4 hours
ahead, ready to bake. The
strudel can be baked up to
a day in advance and
served cold.

Freeze:
The uncooked strudel
freezes well.

Mary's Classic Tip:
* It's best to cool the strudel
  a little before drizzling with
  icing so that it doesn't melt.

An apple strudel used to be such a popular recipe and we think it's worth a bold comeback. Crisp pastry layers with soft fruit inside, the lemon icing adds zing to the flavour. An updated edition is to add breadcrumbs. These help to absorb some of the liquid from the apples and stops the pastry going soggy. Folding in the ends of the pastry first forms neat ends.

1. Preheat the oven to 190°C/170°C fan/Gas 5 and lightly grease a baking tray with butter.

2. First prepare the filling. Place the apple and pear slices in a large bowl, add the lemon juice and zest, sugar and mixed spice and mix together to combine.

3. Lay three sheets of filo pastry on a large board lined with baking paper (see tip on page 158). Place them side by side with the long edges together and slightly overlapping in the middle where they join. Brush with melted butter. Place another three filo sheets on top, laying them crossways over the layer beneath and with the sheets slightly overlapping, as before. Brush with more melted butter, then sprinkle the breadcrumbs over the pastry.

4. Spoon the filling along the bottom third of one long edge of the pastry, leaving a gap of about 5cm (2in) from the long edge and shorter sides. Fold the shorter sides of the pastry over the filling and roll up the strudel from the filling end into a sausage shape with the join underneath. Brush all over with the remaining melted butter and carefully lift the paper and strudel on to the greased baking tray.

5. Bake for 30–35 minutes until the pastry is golden and crisp all over, then remove and leave to cool down a little (see tip).

6. Blend the lemon juice with the icing sugar to make a thick icing, then drizzle over the top of the strudel. Transfer to a serving plate using a fish slice and serve with cream.

Step-by-step images overleaf →

Making the Pear & Apple Strudel:

Bread & Butter Pudding

SERVES 6 / COOK TIME: 25–30 minutes, plus soaking and standing

100g (4oz) sultanas
2 tbsp brandy (see tip)
50g (2oz) butter, softened, plus extra for greasing
8 medium slices of white bread
3 eggs
300ml (10fl oz) milk
150ml (5fl oz) double cream
½ tsp vanilla extract
75g (3oz) caster sugar
25g (1oz) demerara sugar
Icing sugar, for dusting

Prepare Ahead:
The sandwiches can be lined up in the dish, then covered in cling film and kept in the fridge for up to a day ahead. The custard can also be made a day ahead and poured over the sandwiches up to an hour before cooking.

Lovely soft, custard-soaked bread with soft, boozy sultanas and a toasty crisp topping. A great dessert for using up slightly stale bread that's passed its best.

1. You will need a 1.8-litre (3¼-pint) shallow ovenproof dish. Grease the dish with a little butter.

2. Measure the sultanas into a bowl and pour over the brandy. Leave to soak in a warm place for about an hour.

3. Spread butter over each slice of bread and sandwich together. Trim off the crusts and discard (see tip), then cut each sandwich into four triangles. You will end up with 16 triangular sandwiches.

4. Arrange the sandwiches in the buttered dish with the pointed ends sticking up. Scatter the soaked sultanas over the top (along with any brandy left in the bowl).

5. Place the eggs in a jug with the milk, cream, vanilla extract and caster sugar and whisk by hand until combined. Pour the custard over the bread and sprinkle with the demerara sugar. If time permits, set aside for between 30 minutes and an hour for the bread to absorb the liquid.

6. Around 10–15 minutes before you are ready to cook, preheat the oven to 200°C/180°C fan/Gas 6.

7. Bake the bread and butter pudding in the oven for about 25–30 minutes until puffed up and golden brown.

8. Dust with icing sugar and serve straight away, with extra cream if you like.

Mary's Classic Tips:
* If there's no brandy to hand, try Calvados or Cointreau.
* Don't throw the crusts away – whizz them into breadcrumbs to freeze for use in other dishes (see tip on page 22).

Apple Tarte Tatin

SERVES 6 / COOK TIME: 40–50 minutes, plus setting and cooling

175g (6oz) granulated sugar

Butter, for greasing

200g (7oz) peeled and cored Bramley apples, diced into 2cm (¾in) chunks

2 tbsp caster sugar

4 large eating apples

Plain flour, for dusting

1 x 375g block of all-butter puff pastry (see tip)

The classic 'upside down' French tart, usually served warm as a pudding. Do not butter the tin before pouring in the caramel otherwise the caramel will be cloudy and not clear.

1. You will need a 23cm (9in) fixed-base cake tin with deep sides.

2. First make the caramel. Measure the granulated sugar and 6 tablespoons of water into a stainless-steel saucepan. Stir gently over a low heat until the sugar has fully dissolved, then remove the spoon and increase the heat. Boil until a golden straw colour (see tip) and immediately pour into the cake tin, letting it spread evenly over the base, then set aside (see tip). Once the caramel has set (after about 30 minutes), butter the tin sides above the caramel line.

3. Meanwhile, place the Bramley apples, caster sugar and 2 tablespoons of water in another saucepan. Stir over a medium heat, then cover with a lid and simmer for about 5–10 minutes until the apples are soft. Remove from the heat, then use a fork to mash the apples to a purée and leave to cool.

4. Preheat the oven to 220°C/200°C fan/Gas 7.

5. Peel and core the eating apples, then thinly slice so they are about 5mm (¼in) thick. Arrange a layer over the caramel in the tin in a circular pattern. Start from the outside of the tin and work inwards, using larger pieces for the outer edge of the circle, and smaller slices for the inner ring. Scatter the remaining apples on top and press down.

6. Add the cooled apple purée in spoonfuls over the sliced apples and carefully spread out in an even layer.

Continued overleaf →

7. On a work surface lightly dusted in flour, roll out the pastry into a circle 2–3cm (¾–1¼in) bigger than the tin. Cover the apples with the pastry and tuck in the edges to make a downward lip. Make a small cross in the top of the pastry with a sharp knife, to let the steam out.

8. Bake in the oven for 35–40 minutes, with a baking tray on the shelf underneath to catch any sugary drips, until the pastry is crisp and golden and the apples are soft.

9. Carefully turn the tarte Tatin out on to a plate and spoon the syrup over the apples. Serve with cream or crème fraîche.

Step-by-step images overleaf →

Prepare Ahead:
Can be made up to 6 hours ahead; leave in the tin to reheat, and turn out to serve.

Mary's Classic Tips:
* If you're short of time, you can use ready-rolled puff pastry, though you may need to roll it out a little more to fit this size of tin.
* It's very important not to let the caramel get too dark or it will taste bitter
* To clean the empty caramel pan, don't attempt to scrub the hardened sugar off – just refill with hot water and pop back on the hob. Bring to the boil and the caramel will melt off and can be poured away. Alternatively, a dishwasher will do the job.

Making the Tarte Tatin:

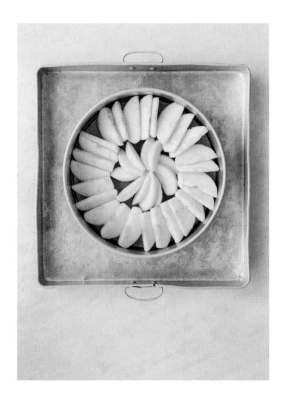

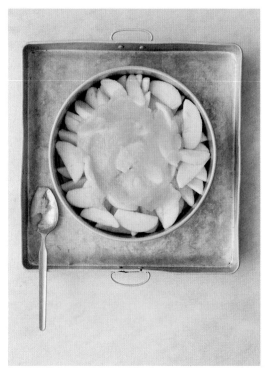

Little Passion Meringue Tartlets

MAKES 8 tartlets / CHILLING TIME: 20 minutes / COOK TIME: 30–33 minutes

For the shortcrust pastry
225g (8oz) plain flour, plus
    extra for dusting
100g (4oz) cold butter,
    cubed, plus extra
    for greasing
25g (1oz) icing sugar
1 egg, beaten

For the filling
6 large ripe passion fruit
    (see tip), halved
3 lemons
75g (3oz) caster sugar
50g (2oz) cornflour
4 egg yolks

For the meringue topping
4 egg whites
225g (8oz) caster sugar

These are simply divine with classic pastry, classic curd and a classic meringue topping. I have sieved the passion fruit seeds, but if you like them you can add them to the filling too so no need to sieve. The tartlets have a lovely contrast of sweet pastry and meringue against the smooth, sharp curd.

1. You will need eight 10cm (4in) round, loose-bottomed tartlet tins with 2.5cm (1in) sides, and a piping bag (optional). Grease the tins.

2. To make the pastry, measure the flour and butter into a food processor and whizz until the mixture is like breadcrumbs. Alternatively, place the flour in a mixing bowl and rub in the butter with your fingertips. Add the icing sugar, egg and 1 tablespoon of water and whizz again until a smooth ball of dough is formed.

3. Divide the dough into eight equal-sized pieces, then roll each out on a floured work surface to the thickness of a £1 coin and slightly larger than the tartlet tins. Carefully line the base and sides of each of the tins, then trim the edges and chill in the fridge for 20 minutes.

4. Preheat the oven to 200°C/180°C fan/Gas 6.

5. Prick the base of each pastry case with a fork, then line with baking paper and baking beans and bake blind for 10 minutes. Remove the paper and beans from the pastry cases and return to the oven to cook for a further 5 minutes until golden and crisp. Set aside to cool.

6. Meanwhile, to make the lemon curd scoop out the juice and pips from the passion fruit and add to a sieve set over a jug. Use a wooden spoon to press the passion fruit pulp through the sieve until you have about 100ml (3½fl oz) of juice (see tip). Add enough lemon juice to make up to 200ml (7fl oz) in total.

7. Measure the sugar, cornflour and 200ml (7fl oz) of water into a saucepan and pour in the passion and lemon juice mixture. Place over a high heat and whisk until thickened and smooth. Remove from the heat, add the egg yolks and whisk again until smooth.

8. Spoon the filling into the pastry cases and level the tops.

9. To make the meringue topping, whisk the egg whites until cloud-like in a grease-free bowl and using an electric hand whisk, then gradually add the sugar, whisking on maximum speed, until the mixture is stiff and glossy. Pipe or spoon the meringue on top of the tarts, spreading it right to the edge of the pastry to cover the curd and seal it in. Return the tarts to the oven to bake for 15–18 minutes until the meringue is lightly cooked and pale golden.

10. Allow the tins to cool to the touch, then push out the tarts, remove the bases and transfer to a serving plate. Serve warm with cream.

Mary's Classic Tips:
* Wrinkled skin is the sign of a ripe passion fruit; smooth-skinned passion fruit are still quite sharp-tasting.
* To extract the maximum juice from the passion fruit seeds, whizz them in a mini food processor before pushing them through the sieve.

Plum Crumble

SERVES 6 / COOK TIME: 30–40 minutes

For the filling
900g (2lb) plums, cut in half
and stones removed
225g (8oz) granulated sugar

For the crumble topping
175g (6oz) plain flour
75g (3oz) cold butter, cubed
50g (2oz) demerara sugar

Prepare Ahead:
Can be assembled up to a
day ahead and kept in the
fridge.

Freeze:
Freezes well assembled
but uncooked.

**My favourite crumble when the trees are laden with fruits.
To make apple crumble, use the same quantity of peeled,
chopped and cored Bramley apples.**

1. You will need a 2-litre (3½-pint) wide-based, shallow
   ovenproof dish. Preheat the oven to 200°C/180°C fan/Gas 6.

2. Put the plum halves and granulated sugar into the dish
   and toss together.

3. Measure the flour and butter into a food processor and
   whizz until the mixture resembles breadcrumbs.
   Alternatively, rub the flour and butter together in a mixing
   bowl with your fingertips. Stir in the demerara sugar and
   sprinkle the mixture evenly over the plums, levelling the top.

4. Place on a baking sheet and bake in the oven for about
   30–40 minutes or until pale golden brown on top and
   bubbling around the edges. Serve with custard, cream
   or crème fraîche.

Step-by-step images overleaf →

Mary's Classic Tip:
* To ring the changes, you could add a teaspoon of ground
  ginger in with crumble topping.

Warm Fondant Brownies

MAKES 16 brownies / COOK TIME: 30–35 minutes, plus cooling

350g (12oz) dark chocolate,
  broken into pieces
250g (9oz) butter, cubed,
  plus extra for greasing
300g (11oz) dark
  muscovado sugar
6 eggs
75g (3oz) ground almonds

....

Prepare Ahead:
Can be made up to a day
ahead and reheated to
serve warm.

....

Freeze:
The cooked brownies
freeze well.

The gooiest of brownies, moist and soft, and ideal as a decadent dessert to serve with ice cream. Wowwee, delicious! These don't contain flour so are perfect for anyone who can't tolerate gluten.

1. You will need a 23 x 30cm (9 x 12in) traybake tin. Preheat the oven to 180°C/160°C fan/Gas 4, then grease the tin with butter and line with baking paper.

2. Place the chocolate in a heatproof bowl, add the butter and set over a small saucepan of gently simmering water. Heat through until runny and melted.

3. Measure the sugar into a bowl, add the eggs and whisk until all the sugar has been incorporated. Carefully pour in the melted chocolate mixture and stir until evenly mixed, then fold in the ground almonds and gently stir to combine.

4. Pour into the prepared tin and bake in the oven for about 30–35 minutes or until a light crust forms on top and the mixture is firm around the edges but still soft in the middle.

5. Leave to cool in the tin, to let the brownies set, then cut into squares (see tip) and serve with ice cream.

Mary's Classic Tip:
* It's best to leave the cooked brownies in the tin, rather than trying to turn them over and peel off the baking paper. They are so gooey, the beautiful crust will be crushed if they are over-handled. Slice straight from the tin, and use a palette knife to remove each square.

Syrup Sponge Pudding

SERVES 8 / COOK TIME: 2–2¼ hours

175g (6oz) golden syrup
175g (6oz) butter, softened,
   plus extra for greasing
125g (4½oz) caster sugar
175g (6oz) self-raising flour
3 eggs
4 tbsp milk

Prepare Ahead:
Can be made up to 8 hours
ahead and gently reheated
to serve.

Freeze:
The cooked sponge
freezes well.

Mary's Classic Tip:
* It's really essential to butter
   the bowl well to help you
   get the pudding out easily.

Steamed pudding is lighter than a suet pudding. The sponge is light and golden and absorbs the syrup to give it a sweet, shiny glaze. Serve with extra warmed syrup if liked.

1. You will need a 1.1-litre (2-pint) pudding basin. Grease the basin with butter (see tip).

2. Measure 75g (3oz) of the golden syrup into the base of the greased basin and 50g (2oz) of the syrup into a mixing bowl. Add the butter to the mixing bowl with the sugar, flour, eggs and milk and beat, either with an electric hand whisk or by hand with a wooden spoon, until light and combined. Spoon the batter into the basin and level the top.

3. Cut a square of foil and a square of baking paper and pleat each in the middle. Place these together, then butter the underside of the baking paper and put the paper-lined foil, buttered side down, on top of the pudding basin. Seal around the edge with string or by tightly crimping the foil.

4. Place a small trivet or upturned flameproof saucer in the bottom of a large deep saucepan and sit the basin on top. Pour in enough boiling water to come halfway up the basin and cover with a tight-fitting lid.

5. Bring back up to the boil, then reduce the heat and simmer very gently for 2–2¼ hours or until the sponge is well risen and firm in the middle. Test with a skewer – if it comes out clean, the sponge is cooked.

6. Carefully remove the basin from the pan and allow to cool a little. To turn out, loosen round the edges with a knife, then turn upside down on to a plate and remove the bowl. Warm the remaining syrup and pour over the top.

7. Serve in wedges with custard, cream or ice cream.

Baked Lemon Curd Cheesecake

SERVES 6 / CHILLING TIME: 15 minutes / COOK TIME: 1 hour, plus cooling

For the base
50g (2oz) butter, plus extra
    for greasing
150g (5oz) digestive biscuits

For the filling
500g (1lb 2oz) full-fat
    mascarpone cheese
300ml (10fl oz) full-fat
    soured cream
150g (5oz) caster sugar
2 eggs
50g (2oz) plain flour
Juice and finely grated zest
    of 2 lemons
3 tbsp lemon curd

For the topping
2 tbsp lemon curd
Lemon balm leaves, to
    decorate (optional)

Prepare Ahead:
Can be made up to a
day ahead.

Freeze:
Freezes well without
the topping.

Made with mascarpone and soured cream, this is a modern twist to the classic. I love the richness and smoothness of using mascarpone and after cooking, the set is soft and creamy.

1. You will need a 20cm (8in) round, spring-form cake tin. Preheat the oven to 180°C/160°C fan/Gas 4, then butter the sides of the tin and line the base with a disc of baking paper.

2. First make the cheesecake base. Melt the butter in a saucepan over a low heat. Place the biscuits in a freezer bag and finely crush with a rolling pin. Tip into the saucepan and stir into the melted butter until the crumbs are coated. Spoon into the base of the prepared tin and use the back of the spoon to press down in an even layer. Chill in the fridge for 15 minutes.

3. To make the filling, measure the mascarpone, soured cream and sugar into a large bowl, add the eggs and mix until smooth with an electric hand whisk. Add the flour and whisk again for 30 seconds, then add the lemon juice, zest and lemon curd and whisk again for few moments until combined. Pour into the tin and level the top.

4. Place on a baking tray and bake in the oven for about an hour until lightly golden around the edges and just set in the middle but with a tiny wobble. Set aside to rest for about 15 minutes, then loosen and remove the sides of the tin and leave to cool completely (see tip). Remove from the base.

5. Transfer the cheesecake to a serving plate. Spread the lemon curd over the top and decorate with lemon balm leaves, if you like, or serve with a few soft summer fruits alongside.

Mary's Classic Tip:
* To help prevent the top of the cheesecake from cracking, once removed from the oven, do not release from the tin too soon.

Rhubarb & White Chocolate Mousse

SERVES 6 / CHILLING TIME: A minimum of 2½ hours / COOK TIME: 5–8 minutes, plus cooling

400g (14oz) pink rhubarb
   stalks, sliced into 1.5cm
   (⅝in) pieces
100g (4oz) caster sugar
125g (4½oz) white chocolate,
   broken into pieces
300ml (10fl oz) double
   cream, at room
   temperature (see tip)
1 tsp vanilla extract

Prepare Ahead:
The mousse be made the day before and chilled in the fridge overnight. The rhubarb can also be made up to a day in advance.

The rhubarb makes a delicate contrast to the white mousse and cuts through the creaminess, but you must use young pink rhubarb, not woody, bitter green rhubarb. The white chocolate sprinkled on top gives a lovely texture. Wonderful served with a ginger thin.

1. You will need six wine glasses of around 150–175ml (5–6fl oz) in capacity.

2. Place the rhubarb and caster sugar in a shallow saucepan and add 2 tablespoons of water. Stir gently over a medium heat for a few minutes until the sugar has dissolved. Cover with a lid, then gently simmer over a medium heat for about 5–8 minutes until tender and just holding its shape. Leave to cool in a bowl, then chill in the fridge for a minimum of 30 minutes.

3. Place 100g (4oz) of the chocolate in a bowl set over a saucepan of gently simmering water and allow to melt. Remove from the heat and leave to cool.

4. Whisk the cream until just before it forms soft peaks. Add the vanilla extract and melted chocolate and gently fold in. The mixture will thicken slightly.

5. Divide the chilled rhubarb among the wine glasses, discarding any excess juice. Spoon the mousse on top of the rhubarb in each glass and swirl the top. Finely chop the remaining chocolate and sprinkle over the mousse, then chill in the fridge for at least 2 hours to allow the mousse to set.

Mary's Classic Tip:
* It's important for the cream to be at room temperature before whisking so that the cream and melted chocolate are each at a similar temperature when combined.

Chocolate & Whisky Cream Roulade

SERVES 8–10 / COOK TIME: 20 minutes, plus cooling

Butter, for greasing
175g (6oz) dark chocolate,
    broken into pieces
175g (6oz) caster sugar
6 eggs, separated
2 tbsp cocoa powder, sifted
Icing sugar, for dusting

For the topping
100g (4oz) dark chocolate,
    broken into pieces
50g (2oz) white chocolate,
    broken into pieces
Cocoa powder, for dusting

For the filling
300ml (10fl oz) double cream
3 tbsp whisky cream liqueur
    such as Baileys or Kahlua

In the past I have always covered the baked roulade with a damp tea towel and left it overnight. Now I find there is no need to do this. Simple, but indulgent and luxurious, and pleasantly alcoholic!

1. You will need a 23 x 33cm (9 x 13in) Swiss roll tin. Preheat the oven to 180°C/160°C fan/Gas 4, then lightly grease the tin with butter and line with baking paper, pushing it right into the corners.

2. First make the sponge. Place the chocolate in a bowl set over a saucepan of gently simmering water, making sure the bowl does not touch the water or the chocolate may overheat. Allow to melt over the heat, then remove from the heat, stir and leave to cool.

3. Place the sugar and egg yolks in a large bowl and whisk with an electric hand whisk until light and creamy. Add the cooled chocolate and stir until evenly blended.

4. In a separate, spotlessly clean bowl, whisk the egg whites into firm peaks but not too stiff. Stir a large spoonful of the egg whites into the chocolate mixture to help loosen it. Mix gently, and then fold in the remaining egg whites, followed by the sifted cocoa powder. Try not to knock out too much air from the egg whites while making sure they are evenly blended.

5. Pour the mixture into the prepared tin and gently level the surface, then bake in the oven for about 20 minutes until firm to the touch. Remove the cooked sponge from the oven and leave in the tin until cold.

Continued overleaf →

6. While the sponge is cooking, prepare the topping. Place the dark and white chocolate in separate bowls, each set over a pan of gently simmering water, and allow to melt. Pour the dark chocolate on to a baking sheet lined with baking paper. Zigzag the white chocolate over the dark chocolate in a random pattern, then leave to set until cold and firm.

7. To make the filling, pour the cream in a bowl and whisk into soft peaks. Stir in the whisky cream.

8. Dust a large sheet of baking paper with icing sugar, then turn the cooled sponge out on to it and peel off the lining paper (see tips). Spread the sponge with the cream, leaving a clear border of around 2cm (¾in) on all sides, as the cream will spread out as the sponge is rolled up. Roll up as tightly as possible, like a Swiss roll, starting from one of the long edges and using the paper to help. Leave the rolled-up sponge wrapped in the paper for a while to help it to hold together. Don't worry if it cracks, though – it adds to the appeal!

9. To finish assembling the roulade, sit the rolled sponge on a long plate with the join underneath, break the sheet of chocolate into large pieces and stick these into the top of the roulade. Dust with cocoa powder and more icing sugar, if you like.

Prepare Ahead:
The roulade can be assembled (without the chocolate topping) up to 8 hours ahead. The chocolate topping can be made up to a day ahead and left somewhere cool to set.

Freeze:
The filled roulade freezes well. Defrost and then decorate with the chocolate topping.

Mary's Classic Tips:
* Lay the baking paper on a clean tea towel to help give extra grip while rolling up the sponge.
* Trim the edges of the sponge before rolling for a neater finish, if you prefer; cut-offs are cook's perks!

Ginger & Rhubarb Chilled Cheesecake

SERVES 8 / CHILLING TIME: A minimum of 4 hours 20 minutes / COOK TIME: 10 minutes, plus cooling

For the base
75g (3oz) butter
150g (5oz) gingernut biscuits

For the filling
2 x 180g tubs of full-fat
   cream cheese
150ml (5fl oz) double cream
6 tbsp ginger syrup (from the
   jar) (see tip)
6 stem ginger bulbs,
   finely chopped

For the topping
300g (11oz) pink rhubarb
   stalks, sliced into 2cm
   (¾in) pieces
150g (5oz) caster sugar
4 sheets of leaf gelatine

Prepare Ahead:
Can be made up to a day
ahead and stored in the fridge.
The rhubarb can also be
made up to a day in advance.

Freeze:
Freezes well.

Mary's Classic Tip:
* Use measuring spoons to
   measure the ginger syrup. If
   too much is added, the filling
   will be too soft and sweet.

It's important to use young pink rhubarb for this recipe – old, woody green rhubarb would not look so pretty!

1. You will need a 20cm (8in) round spring-form tin with deep sides. Line the sides with strips of cling film (using a little water to help the cling film stick) and then line the base with a disc of baking paper.

2. First make the cheesecake base. Melt the butter in a saucepan over a low heat. Place the biscuits in a freezer bag and finely crush with a rolling pin. Tip into the pan and stir into the butter until the crumbs are coated. Spoon into the base of the tin and press down evenly. Chill for at least 20 minutes.

3. To make the filling, measure the cream cheese, cream and ginger syrup into a large bowl. Beat using an electric hand whisk until very stiff and smooth. Stir in the chopped ginger, then spoon into the tin, spreading it over the biscuit layer and levelling the top. Chill in the fridge for about an hour.

4. To make the topping, place the rhubarb and sugar in a shallow pan and add 3 tablespoons of water. Stir over a medium heat for a few minutes until the sugar has dissolved. Cover with a lid, then simmer over a medium heat for 5–8 minutes until the rhubarb is tender and just holding its shape. Remove and leave to cool, reserving half the rhubarb to serve with the cheesecake. (Place in a bowl and chill.)

5. Soak the gelatine leaves in a bowl of cold water for about 5 minutes until squidgy and gel-like. Squeeze out the water and add the gelatine to the rhubarb in the pan, gently stirring until the gelatine has completely dissolved. Leave to cool, then pour over the cream cheese layer in the tin and spread the rhubarb pieces out evenly. Chill in the fridge for a minimum of 3 hours.

6. Remove the sides of the tin and carefully peel away the cling film, then slip the baking paper base from underneath the cheesecake. Transfer to a serving plate, cut into wedges and serve with the reserved compote on the side.

Apricot & Brandy Ice Cream Bombe

SERVES 8–10 / COOK TIME: 5 minutes, plus cooling / FREEZING TIME: A minimum of 12 hours

6 tbsp brandy

250g (9oz) ready-to-eat dried apricots, cut into tiny pieces

Juice and finely grated zest of 1 orange

4 eggs, separated

100g (4oz) caster sugar

300ml (10fl oz) double cream

100g (4oz) amaretti biscuits, roughly crumbled

Freeze:

Can be kept in the freezer for up to a month.

Mary's Classic Tips:

* Use a good length of cling film to line the pudding basin; you will need plenty of 'overhang' at the edges to get a good grip when un-moulding the frozen pudding later. If your cling film is a thinner variety, try doubling up and using two layers, to prevent it tearing.

* Take care when unmoulding the ice cream bombe; leaving it at room temperature for a few minutes before serving will make it easier to remove the cling film in one piece, so there are no little rogue torn pieces left in the dessert.

Perfect for any celebration over the festive season – in the freezer, ready to serve. If you don't have brandy in the cupboard, you could use an alternative such as amaretto.

1. You will need a 1.75-litre (3-pint) pudding basin, lined with cling film (see tip).

2. Place the brandy, apricots, orange juice and zest in a saucepan. Stir together and cook over a medium heat for 2–3 minutes, then bring to the boil and boil for a minute. Cover with a lid and set aside to cool down completely.

3. Place the egg whites in a large grease-free bowl and use an electric hand whisk to beat until stiff and fluffy like a cloud. Gradually add the sugar, a little at a time, still whisking at maximum speed, until all the sugar has been incorporated and the mixture is stiff and glossy. Beat the egg yolks in a separate bowl and carefully fold into the egg whites until the mixture is evenly coloured and streak-free.

4. Whip the cream to soft peaks, then fold into the egg mixture until combined. Add the apricot mixture (including any liquid) from the pan. Add most of the chopped amaretti (reserving about a fifth of them) and stir until just combined – do not beat or over-mix. Spoon into the lined pudding basin, cover the top with cling film and freeze for a minimum of 12 hours.

5. Shortly before serving, remove the pudding basin from the freezer and allow the ice cream to sit at room temperature for a few minutes, then turn upside down on to a serving plate, carefully remove the basin and peel off the cling film (see tip). Sprinkle with the remaining amaretti biscuits to serve.

Step-by-step images overleaf →

Making the Apricot & Brandy Ice Cream Bombe:

Banoffee Pie

SERVES 8–12 / CHILLING TIME: A minimum of 2¼ hours / COOK TIME: 5 minutes

For the base
150g (5oz) digestive biscuits
   (about 10)
75g (3oz) butter

For the filling (see tip)
75g (3oz) butter
75g (3oz) light
   muscovado sugar
1 x 397g tin of full-fat
   condensed milk
1 tsp vanilla extract

For the topping
3 small just-ripe bananas
300ml (10fl oz) double cream
50g (2oz) dark chocolate,
   broken into pieces, or
   1 tbsp cocoa powder

Prepare Ahead:
The base and filling can be made up to a day ahead and kept in the fridge. Ideally, the pie should be assembled with the banana and cream on the day. However, it can be assembled a day in advance: as long as the banana is completely covered in the cream, it will not discolour.

Mary's Classic Tip:
* For a speedier dessert, use a tin of ready-made caramel (bear in mind this doesn't set as firmly).

Life before banoffee pie seems prehistoric as it is such a loved dessert! I have made it as a salted caramel banoffee (add a teaspoon of sea salt), though I prefer the classic version. Full of calories and no apologies!

1. You will need a 20cm (8in) round, spring-form tin with deep sides, and a piping bag (optional). Line the sides of the tin with strips of cling film (using a little water to help the cling film stick) and then line the base with a disc of baking paper.

2. First make the pie base. Place the biscuits in a freezer bag and finely crush with a rolling pin. Melt the butter in a non-stick saucepan over a low heat, add the biscuits and combine. Spoon into the base of the tin, pressing down with the back of the spoon to level. Chill for 15 minutes.

3. To make the filling, heat the butter and sugar in the same pan and stir over a low heat until combined. Add the condensed milk and bring to the boil and boil, stirring continuously, for 2–3 minutes or until dark golden, taking care that the mixture doesn't catch on the bottom. Do not allow to boil for too long or it will become grainy. Add the vanilla extract and pour into the tin. Chill in the fridge for a minimum of 1 hour or up to 24 hours.

4. Peel and slice the bananas and arrange in neat rounds on top of the caramel. Whip the cream to soft peaks and spoon or pipe it over the bananas, then level the top before chilling in the fridge for an hour.

5. Meanwhile, melt the chocolate in a bowl set over pan of gently simmering water. Remove from the heat and allow to cool.

6. Remove the edges of the tin from the banoffee pie, peel off the cling film and transfer to a serving plate, slipping the baking paper from underneath. Zigzag the melted chocolate over the top (if using), making sure it's cool or it will melt the cream, or dust with cocoa powder.

Step-by-step images overleaf →

Making the Banoffee Pie:

Plum Ice Cream

SERVES 8 / COOK TIME: 15–20 minutes, plus cooling / FREEZING TIME: A minimum of 6 hours

800g (1¾lb) plums (such as
Victoria), cut in half and
stones removed
100g (4oz) caster sugar
8 sprigs of mint, to decorate

For the ice-cream base
4 eggs, separated
100g (4oz) caster sugar
300ml (10fl oz) double cream

Prepare Ahead:
The purée can be made up to
a week ahead and stored in
the fridge.

Freeze:
The ice cream can be kept
in the freezer for up to
2 months. The purée can also
be frozen.

Mary's Classic Tips:
* If space is restricted in your
freezer, use two smaller
containers instead.
* For a pretty variation,
ripple the plum purée
through the ice cream
before freezing.

Ice cream is classic, but my technique is not classic – that would be making a custard. I prefer to make it with a soft meringue base and then there is no need to use an ice cream machine. We have an abundance of plums on our trees around August time so I stock up on making this ice cream.

1. You will need a 1.5–2-litre (2 ½–3½-pint) freezer-proof container with a lid (see tip).

2. Place the plums in a wide-based saucepan, add the sugar and stir gently over a medium heat for 3–4 minutes until the sugar has dissolved. Cover with a lid and gently stew for 10–15 minutes or until the plums have broken down.

3. Tip the stewed plums into a sieve set over a measuring jug and use a wooden spoon to push the plums through the sieve to remove the skins and any stray stones. Set the purée aside to cool.

4. Next make the ice cream. Whisk the egg whites in a large bowl with an electric hand whisk until stiff and like a cloud. Gradually add the sugar, whisking on maximum speed, until it is fully incorporated and the mixture forms soft peaks but is not too stiff.

5. In a separate bowl, whisk the cream into soft peaks. Stir in the egg yolks and about 200ml (7fl oz) of the plum purée until combined (see tip). Add a large tablespoon of the egg white mixture and mix in to loosen, then fold in the remainder of the egg whites, making sure that they are evenly incorporated.

6. Spoon into the freezer-proof container and freeze for a minimum of 6 hours or overnight.

7. To serve, remove from the freezer and leave at room temperature for a short while to make scooping easier. Spoon into bowls, pour over a little plum purée and add a sprig of mint to decorate.

Light Raspberry Mousse

SERVES 6–8 / CHILLING TIME: A minimum of 4 hours

4 sheets of leaf gelatine
300g (11oz) raspberries, plus
  extra to decorate
4 eggs, separated
75g (3oz) caster sugar
150ml (5fl oz) double cream
Sprigs of mint, to decorate

Prepare Ahead:
The mousse can be made up
to 8 hours ahead and kept in
the fridge.

Mary's Classic Tip:
* It is important to keep
  folding the whipped cream
  into the raspberry mixture
  until smooth and evenly
  coloured throughout and
  no lumps remain, otherwise
  the resulting mousse will
  be flecked with spots of
  white cream.

So full of flavour – close your eyes and you could be in a field of raspberries on a summer's day! A beautiful, dusty pink-coloured mousse, light, soft and airy with no dreaded lumps of gelatine.

1. You will need a large glass bowl (1.1 litres/2 pints) or six to eight dessert glasses.

2. Soak the gelatine in a small heatproof bowl of cold water for 5 minutes until soft. Squeeze out the liquid from the gelatine and tip away all but 1 tablespoon of water. Put the gelatine back into the bowl with the reserved tablespoon of water. Set the bowl on top of a saucepan of gently simmering water and stir for a few minutes until the gelatine is dissolved and runny. Remove from the heat and set aside to keep warm.

3. Whizz the raspberries in a food processor until blended to a smooth pulp. Place in a sieve above a bowl and push the pulp through with a metal spoon to remove the seeds.

4. Place the egg yolks and caster sugar in a large bowl. Use an electric hand whisk to whisk the eggs and sugar for 4–5 minutes or until thick, pale and fluffy and when you lift up the whisk, a trail is left in the mixture. Stir in the raspberry purée, followed by the runny gelatine.

5. Whip the cream to soft peaks, then carefully fold into the raspberry mixture (see tip). In a clean, dry bowl, whisk the egg whites until stiff. Stir 2 tablespoons of the egg whites into the raspberry mixture, then gently fold in the remaining egg whites.

6. Spoon into the large glass bowl or divide among the individual glasses, then chill in the fridge for a minimum of 4 hours until set. Serve straight from the fridge, decorated with the remaining raspberries and sprigs of mint.

Step-by-step images overleaf →

Making the Light Raspberry Mousse:

Chocolate Truffle Pots

MAKES 6 pots / CHILLING TIME: A minimum of 6 hours

For the chocolate mousse
100g (4oz) dark chocolate,
    broken into pieces
50g (2oz) caster sugar
2 egg yolks
1 tbsp whisky cream liqueur,
    e.g. Baileys
300ml (10fl oz) double cream

For the truffle balls
4 digestive biscuits
1–2 tbsp whisky cream
    liqueur, e.g. Baileys
100g (4oz) white chocolate,
    broken into pieces
Cocoa powder, for dusting

Prepare Ahead:
The mousse and truffle balls
can be made up to a day
ahead and kept in the fridge.

Freeze:
Both the mousse and the
truffle balls freeze well.

**Velvety smooth, light and chocolatey, the mousse is divine.
The truffle on the top gives an extra crunch – buy them if you
would rather not make them! Use a whisky cream liqueur or
any chocolate or coffee cream liqueur of your choice.**

1. You will need six small wine glasses, sundae glasses or
   ceramic pots.

2. Place the dark chocolate in a food processor and process
   for 1 minute or until just a few pieces remain in the
   otherwise powdery chocolate mixture. Alternatively, finely
   grate the chocolate.

3. Measure the sugar and 6 tablespoons of water into a small
   saucepan and heat gently, stirring until the sugar has
   dissolved. Raise the heat and boil briskly for a few seconds
   until the liquid has become a thin syrup.

4. Set the food processor running and carefully pour in the hot
   syrup through the feed tube on to the chocolate so it melts
   and becomes liquid. Add just a little more boiling water if
   some unmelted chocolate remains. Add the egg yolks and
   process for a few seconds before adding the whisky cream
   liqueur. If you are not using a food processor, add the hot
   syrup to the chocolate to melt it before beating the
   ingredients together.

5. In a separate bowl, whip the cream to soft peaks, then fold in
   the chocolate mixture. Reserve 3 tablespoons of the mousse
   in a medium bowl before spooning the rest into the glasses.
   Place in the fridge to set for 6 hours or overnight.

Continued overleaf →

6. Meanwhile make the truffle balls. Place the biscuits in a
    freezer bag and finely crush with a rolling pin. Add the
    crushed biscuits to the reserved mousse, followed by the
    whisky cream liqueur. Mix well and shape into six balls,
    each about the size of a small walnut, then place in the
    fridge to set for 10–15 minutes.

7. Melt the white chocolate in a small bowl set over a pan of
    gently simmering water. Insert a cocktail stick into each of
    the balls, then dip into the melted chocolate and swirl
    around until coated. Place on a piece of baking paper and
    chill in the fridge for 30 minutes until firm.

8. Remove the chocolate pots from the fridge just before
    serving (see tip), place a truffle ball on top of each one
    and dust with a little cocoa powder.

Mary's Classic Tip:
* It's important to keep the
   chocolate pots in the fridge
   right up until serving as
   they become runny if left
   out at room temperature.

Crème Brûlée

SERVES 6 / COOK TIME: 25–30 minutes / CHILLING TIME: A minimum of 4 hours

Butter, for greasing
4 large egg yolks
50g (2oz) caster sugar
1 tsp vanilla extract
300ml (10fl oz) single cream
300ml (10fl oz) double cream
50g (2oz) demerara sugar

Prepare Ahead:
Can be made up to 4 hours
ahead (kept at room
temperature). The custard
base can be made up to a
day ahead.

Mary's Classic Tips:
* Try to pour the custard mix
  into the ramekins without
  splashing, otherwise the
  splashes will burn on the
  sides of the ramekins
  during cooking, when
  you're aiming for a
  beautiful clean finish.
* If grilling the tops of the
  brûlées, stand all the dishes
  on a very flat, sturdy baking
  sheet – one that will not
  buckle under the heat of
  the grill. This will make
  it easy to slide them in
  and out of the hot grill in
  one go, and the sugar will
  melt evenly.

Often made with full double cream, I prefer to add some single cream to make it slightly less heavy. The custard should be smooth with not a bubble in sight.

1. You will need six 125ml (4fl oz) ramekins. Preheat the oven to 160°C/140°C fan/Gas 3 and grease the ramekins with a little butter.

2. Place the egg yolks in a large bowl, add the caster sugar and vanilla extract and whisk together by hand.

3. Heat the single and double cream together in a saucepan until hand hot, then gradually pour into the bowl with the egg yolk mixture, whisking until combined. Pour the mixture through a sieve into a large jug, to strain out any lumps, then carefully pour into the ramekins, dividing the mixture evenly among them (see tip).

4. Put the ramekins into a small roasting tin lined with kitchen paper or a folded cloth (to prevent the dishes from moving around in the tray), then pour enough boiling water into the tin to come halfway up the sides of the ramekins.

5. Carefully slide the tin into the oven and bake for about 25–30 minutes or until nearly set but with a slight wobble in the middle. Leave to cool in the tin, then transfer to the fridge to chill until set for 4 hours or overnight.

6. When ready to serve, sprinkle the demerara sugar on top of the custard in an even layer. Using a blowtorch, heat the tops until caramelised and golden brown, or caramelise the tops under a hot grill (see tip).

7. Serve as soon as the caramel has cooled and become brittle.

Lemon Soufflé Pudding

SERVES 6 / COOK TIME: 30–35 minutes

100g (4oz) butter, softened, plus extra for greasing
175g (6oz) caster sugar
Juice and finely grated zest of 3 lemons
4 large eggs, separated
75g (3oz) plain flour
450ml (15fl oz) full-fat milk

This is one of my most favourite hot puddings – sometimes called Magic Lemon Pudding as it has a lemon sauce hidden under the sponge.

1. You will need a 1.8-litre (3¼-pint) wide-based, shallow ovenproof dish. Preheat the oven to 180°C/160°C fan/Gas 4 and grease the dish with butter.

2. Measure the butter and sugar into a bowl and whisk with an electric hand whisk until pale and creamy. Add the lemon juice and zest and whisk again until combined. Whisk in the yolks and half the flour and then add the remaining flour, wiping down the sides of the bowl with a spatula in between to incorporate every last bit of mixture. Pour in the milk a little at a time and whisk until the mix looks slightly curdled.

3. Whisk the egg whites in a clean, grease-free bowl until they look like a cloud (see tip). Add 1 heaped tablespoon of the egg whites to the batter, mix well and then fold in the remaining whites until you have a smooth mixture.

4. Gently pour the finished batter into the prepared dish (see tip), then place in a large roasting tin and fill with enough boiling water to come halfway up the dish.

5. Carefully place in the oven and bake for 30–35 minutes until lightly golden and well risen, with a slight wobble in the centre. Serve at once.

Mary's Classic Tips:
* Don't forget to wash the beaters of the electric whisk before whisking the egg whites. Like the mixing bowl, they must be clean and completely grease-free or the whites will not whip.
* When the batter is made, it is important to pour it into the ovenproof dish carefully to make sure that none of the air that has been incorporated by whisking is knocked out. Lift the dish gently, trying not to knock or bang it down, to ensure that air bubbles don't escape from the batter.

Lemon Syllabub

SERVES 6 / CHILLING TIME: A minimum of 2 hours

1 lemon (see tip)
100ml (3½fl oz) sweet
   white wine
75g (3oz) caster sugar
300ml (10fl oz) pouring
   double cream

....

Prepare Ahead:
Can be made up to 24 hours
ahead and stored in the
fridge.

A forgotten favourite, so easy to do, especially for entertaining – delicate and spoiling.

1. You will need six martini glasses or small ceramic pots.

2. Use a vegetable peeler to thinly peel the lemon rind into long, thick strips, taking care not to cut too much of the bitter white pith, and then halve the lemon to squeeze out the juice.

3. Put the wine, lemon rind and juice in a saucepan and add the sugar. Heat gently, stirring, until the sugar has dissolved, then remove from the heat and set aside to cool for a minimum of 1 hour to allow the flavours to infuse. Alternatively, leave to infuse overnight.

4. Strain the syrup into a bowl. Retain some of the lemon peel (now nicely candied from being infused in the syrup) and cut into fine strips.

5. Pour the cream into the same bowl and whisk until it has thickened and is just holding its shape. Divide among the martini glasses or small pots (see tip) and chill in the fridge for a minimum of 2 hours. Decorate with the strips of candied lemon peel and serve chilled.

Step-by-step images overleaf →

Mary's Classic Tips:
* Choose an unwaxed lemon as the lemon peel is an integral part of this recipe. If you can't find one, make sure you give your lemon a good scrub under running water before use.
* Take your time filling the serving glasses. Use a dessertspoon to carefully fill them, letting each dollop fall gently into the middle of the glass. There is no need to level the top of the syllabub – simply leave with a lovely rounded surface. Wipe the edges of the glass free of any little drips before serving.

Making the Lemon Syllabub:

Summer Berry Pavlova

SERVES 8 / COOK TIME: 1–1½ hours, plus cooling

For the pavlova
6 large egg whites
375g (13oz) caster sugar
1 tsp white wine vinegar
1 tsp cornflour

For the topping
300ml (10fl oz) double cream
300g (11oz) natural Greek-
   style yoghurt
1 tsp vanilla extract
50g (2oz) icing sugar, sifted,
   plus extra for dusting
500g (1lb 2oz) mixed
   summer fruits (such as
   blueberries, raspberries
   and strawberries)

Beyond a classic; more of an institution! A lovely crowd pleaser and an easy, prepare-ahead dessert for entertaining.

1. Preheat the oven to 160°C/140°C fan/Gas 3. Line a baking sheet with baking paper and draw a 15cm (6in) circle in the centre of the paper and a 30cm (12oz) circle around the outside to make a ring.

2. Place the egg whites in a large, spotlessly clean bowl and whisk with an electric hand whisk until stiff and cloud-like (see tip). Gradually add the sugar, whisking on maximum speed, and mix until stiff and glossy (see tip). You may need to scrape down the sides of the bowl with a spatula from time to time. Place the vinegar and cornflour in a cup and mix into a smooth paste, then add to the meringue and stir to combine.

3. Spoon the meringue mixture into the ring marked on the baking paper (see tip). Using the back of a dessertspoon, make a trench all the way around the top of the meringue ring.

4. Slide the baking sheet into the oven and immediately reduce the temperature to 140°C/120°C fan/Gas 1. Cook the meringue ring for 1–1½ hours or until firm to the touch. Turn the oven off and leave the meringue inside to cool for about 2 hours.

Continued overleaf →

5. To assemble, whip the cream into soft peaks, gently stir in the yoghurt, vanilla extract and icing sugar and spoon into the trench of the meringue ring. Arrange all the mixed fruit on top and dust with icing sugar. Cut into wedges to serve.

Prepare Ahead:
Once cooked, the meringue can be kept in a cool place for up to 2 weeks ahead, then topped with the cream and fruit 4 hours before serving.

Mary's Classic Tips:

* A good test to check if the egg whites are whipped enough before adding the sugar, is to tip the bowl slightly. If the egg whites stay put, they are ready; if they start to slip, and would slide out of the bowl, they need a little more whisking.
* If you have a free-standing food mixer, use it to make the meringue as it will carry on whisking while you gradually add the sugar.
* Keep the shaped meringue ring from sliding off the baking sheet on the way to and from the oven by sticking the baking paper down with a little of the meringue mix. Put a little blob of the raw meringue underneath each corner of the paper, to glue it to the baking sheet. If cooking in a fan oven, this also stops the edges of the paper from blowing up against the soft meringue as it cooks.

Panna Cotta with Pineapple & Ginger

SERVES 6 / COOK TIME: 5 minutes / CHILLING TIME: A minimum of 6 hours

For the panna cotta
Sunflower oil, for greasing
6 sheets of leaf gelatine
600ml (1 pint) single cream
300ml (10fl oz) double cream
75g (3oz) caster sugar
1 tbsp vanilla extract

For the sweet salsa
Flesh of 1 small ripe
    pineapple (about
    200g/7oz), cut into
    5mm (¼in) dice
4 stem ginger bulbs
    (about 75g/3oz), cut
    into 5mm (¼in) dice
6 tbsp ginger syrup
    (from the jar)

Prepare Ahead:
The panna cotta and salsa
can both be made up to
2 days ahead and kept in
the fridge.

I love the classic vanilla panna cotta, but adding the ginger and pineapple gives it a fresh punch. Smooth, creamy panna cotta with the perfect wobble!

1. You will need six 150–175ml (5–6fl oz) metal pudding basins (timbale moulds). Oil the inside of each mould with sunflower oil, then leave upside down to drain on kitchen paper to remove any excess oil.

2. To make the panna cotta, soak the gelatine leaves in a small bowl of cold water for about 5 minutes or until soft.

3. Pour the single and double creams into a saucepan, add the sugar and gently bring to the boil, stirring to dissolve the sugar, until just scalding (about to boil). Immediately remove from the heat.

4. Remove the gelatine from the water and squeeze to get rid of any excess water. Add to the warm cream and stir until the gelatine has completely dissolved. Stir in the vanilla extract and pour into a jug (see tip). Divide the mixture among the oiled moulds, pouring almost to the top. Allow to cool a little, then cover with cling film and chill in the fridge for a minimum of 6 hours, or ideally overnight, until set and firm to the touch.

5. To make the salsa, mix all the ingredients together in a bowl.

6. Carefully turn out each panna cotta and invert it into the centre of a small plate (see tip). Spoon the salsa on top and around the edges to serve.

Mary's Classic Tips:
* There is a lot of cream, so you may find it easier to split it into two batches, pouring it out a half at a time to avoid spilling it.
* To turn a panna cotta out of its mould easily, dip the base in hot water for a few moments until the panna cotta loosens in the mould, then invert on a serving plate.

Freshest of Fresh Fruit Salad

SERVES 6

Flesh of 1 cantaloupe melon,
cut into 2cm (¾in) cubes
2 kiwi fruit, peeled, halved
and sliced into crescents
1 mango, peeled and diced
250g (9oz) seedless green
grapes, halved
1 x 435g tin of lychees (see
tip), drained and syrup
reserved
2 passion fruit
Finely grated zest and juice
of 1 small lime

....

Prepare Ahead:
Can be made up to 8 hours
ahead and then stored in
the fridge.

This makes a change from a red fruit salad; I love the freshness of the green and orange fruits and lime. It is classic to serve it in a bowl but try, for a change, to arrange the fruits on a platter.

1. Place the melon, kiwi fruit, mango, grapes and lychees in a bowl and mix together.

2. Cut the passion fruit in half and scoop out the seeds and juice into a separate bowl. Add the reserved lychee syrup with the lime zest and juice. Mix together and pour over the fruit salad.

Mary's Classic Tip:
* The lychees add a lovely perfumed flavour to the fruit salad. If you're not keen on them whole, slice them into smaller pieces.

TEATIME

English Muffins

MAKES 12–14 muffins / PROVING TIME: 2 hours 20 minutes / COOK TIME: 30 minutes

350g (12oz) strong white
   flour, plus extra for dusting
25g (1oz) butter, softened
1 x 7g packet of fast-action
   dried yeast
1 tbsp caster sugar
1 tsp salt
1 large egg, beaten
175ml (6fl oz) milk
A little oil, for greasing

Prepare Ahead:
Can be made up to 8 hours
ahead. Any left over are good
toasted the next day.

Freeze:
The muffins freeze well.
Once defrosted, refresh
in a low oven to serve.

Mary's Classic Tip:
* Make sure the pastry cutter
   is well dusted with flour to
   make it easier to cut out the
   muffins without squashing
   the sides. Don't twist the
   cutter – just press firmly,
   then lift it up and push the
   dough out gently.

If you do not have two frying pans, leave the second batch of muffins in the fridge until the first ones are cooked. A flat griddle pan could also be used.

1. You will need a 6cm (2½in) plain pastry cutter.

2. Measure the flour and butter into the bowl of a free-standing food mixer and whizz together until the mixture resembles breadcrumbs. Alternatively, rub together with your fingertips in a mixing bowl. Add the yeast to one side of the bowl, then place the sugar and salt on the other side. Add the egg and milk and mix together, either in the machine, using the dough hook, or by hand. Knead on a low speed for about 7 minutes, or by hand for around 10 minutes, until you have smooth, shiny dough.

3. Grease a large bowl with oil. Add the dough, cover with cling film and leave to rise for 2 hours or until doubled in size.

4. Tip the dough on to a floured work surface and knead for a minute or so to lightly knock back, then roll out to a rough rectangle 2–2.5cm (¾–1in) thick. Dust the pastry cutter with flour and stamp out as many rounds as you can (see tip). Knead any leftover dough together as smoothly as possible, then cut out more until the dough is used up. It should make 12–14 rounds, depending on how thick you roll it.

5. Place the muffins on a lined or floured baking sheet. Cover with cling film and leave to prove for 20 minutes until fluffy.

6. Preheat the oven to 180°C/160°C fan/Gas 4.

7. Heat two large frying pans or a flat griddle pan over a very low heat. Add the muffins and cook for 8 minutes each side until a golden crust forms on the top and bottom. Return to the baking sheet and bake in the oven for 10–12 minutes or until lightly golden and the sides of the muffins are firm and no longer have a doughy appearance. Transfer to a wire rack to cool and serve either cold or warm and spread with butter.

Step-by-step images overleaf →

Making the English Muffins:

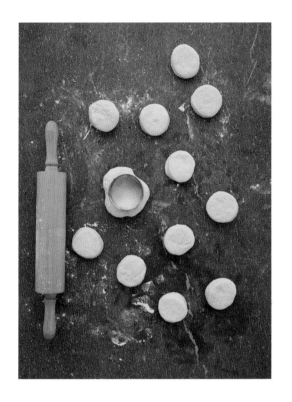

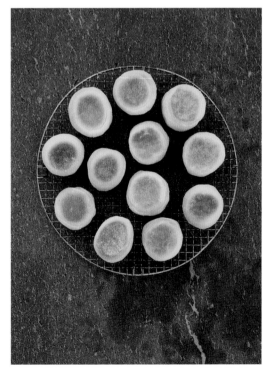

Classic Flapjacks

MAKES **24 flapjacks** / COOK TIME: **30 minutes, plus cooling**

150g (5oz) butter, cubed,
  plus extra for greasing
150g (5oz) muscovado sugar
150g (5oz) golden syrup
1 tsp vanilla extract
225g (8oz) rolled oats

Prepare Ahead:
Can be made up to 3 days
ahead and stored in an
airtight container.

Freeze:
These freeze well.

**Adored by all ages and perfect for the biscuit tin. I like them
with a little softness in the centre, not too brittle.**

1. You will need an 18cm (7in) square, solid-based baking tin
   with deep sides. Preheat the oven to 180°C/160°C fan/
   Gas 4, then grease the tin with butter and line the base with
   a square of baking paper.

2. Measure the butter, sugar and syrup into a saucepan (see
   tip). Slowly melt over a low heat, stirring until the butter is
   melted and the sugar has dissolved. Remove from the heat,
   then add the vanilla extract and rolled oats and stir to combine.

3. Spoon into the prepared tin and level the top, then bake
   in the oven for about 30 minutes or until firm to the touch
   around the edges but still a little soft in the centre. Leave
   to cool in the tin for about 20 minutes.

4. Turn out, remove the baking paper and cut into 24 pieces.

Mary's Classic Tip:
∗ Golden syrup is readily available in squeezy bottles, which
   makes it easy to measure out. If it's in the traditional tin,
   use a greased spoon for measuring so that it slips off easily.

Victoria Sandwich

SERVES 6–8 / COOK TIME: 25 minutes, plus cooling

225g (8oz) cold baking
    spread, plus extra
    for greasing
225g (8oz) caster sugar,
    plus extra for sprinkling
225g (8oz) self-raising flour
2 level tsp baking powder
4 eggs

For the filling
150ml (5fl oz) double cream
About 4 tbsp strawberry or
    raspberry jam

Prepare Ahead:
Can be made and assembled
up to 8 hours ahead.

Freeze:
The cooked sponges
freeze well.

A great British classic. The all-in-one method makes it one of the simplest cakes to make, but it looks really impressive. The classic version has just jam, but I like to add whipped cream too to make it extra special. I made it as part of a tennis tea and it was welcomed with lots of complimentary oohs and ahhs!

1. You will need two 20cm (8in) round, loose-bottomed sandwich tins with deep sides. Preheat the oven to 180°C/160°C fan/Gas 4, then lightly grease the tins and line each base with a disc of baking paper.

2. Measure the baking spread, sugar, flour and baking powder into a large bowl, add the eggs and, using either a wooden spoon or an electric hand whisk, beat for about 2 minutes until just blended. Divide the mixture evenly between the prepared tins and level the tops.

3. Bake in the oven for about 25 minutes or until well risen and golden. The tops of the sponges should spring back when pressed lightly with a finger. Leave to cool in the tins for around 10 minutes until cool to the touch, then run a blunt knife around the edge of the tins to free the sides of the sponges. Turn the cakes out, then peel off the baking paper and leave to cool completely on a wire rack (see tip).

4. Whip the cream into soft peaks, then choose the cake with the best top and place the other sponge, top side down, on a serving plate. Spread with the jam and the whipped cream. Sit the other cake on top (top side up) and sprinkle with caster sugar to serve.

Mary's Classic Tip:
* To avoid unsightly marks on the top of the cakes, place each
   sponge bottom side down on the wire rack.

White Chocolate, Cherry & Brandy Celebration Cake

SERVES 8 / COOK TIME: 25–35 minutes, plus cooling

100g (4oz) white chocolate, broken into pieces (see tip)
225g (8oz) butter, softened, plus extra for greasing
250g (9oz) self-raising flour
225g (8oz) caster sugar
½ tsp vanilla extract
4 eggs

For the filling and topping
450ml (15fl oz) double cream
2–3 tbsp brandy
1–2 tbsp icing sugar, sifted
150g (5oz) good cherry jam
100g (4oz) white chocolate (see tip)

Adding white chocolate gives a lovely moist sponge, while the cherry and brandy give a touch of luxury for a special occasion.

1. You will need two 20cm (8in) round, loose-bottomed sandwich tins and a large piping bag with a large star nozzle. Preheat the oven to 180°C/160°C fan/Gas 4, then grease the tins with the butter and line each base with a disc of baking paper.

2. Place the white chocolate for the sponge in a bowl set over a small saucepan of gently simmering water (making sure the water does not come into direct contact with the bowl) and stir until melted. Set aside to cool.

3. To make the sponges, measure the butter and flour into a large bowl with the sugar and vanilla extract. Add the eggs and beat with an electric hand whisk until light and smooth. Stir in the slightly cooled melted chocolate and whisk again for a moment until incorporated. Divide between the prepared the tins and level the tops.

4. Bake in the oven for 25–35 minutes until golden, well risen and just shrinking away from the sides of the tin. Allow to cool in the tins for 15–20 minutes, then once the tins are cold enough to handle, remove the cakes and place on a wire rack to cool down fully. Remove the lining paper from each sponge.

Prepare Ahead:
The sponges can be made up to a day ahead. Assemble up to 6 hours ahead and serve at room temperature.

....

Freeze:
The sponges freeze well (without the topping).

5. Meanwhile, make the filling and topping. Whip the cream into soft peaks and fold in the brandy and icing sugar. Sit one cake upside down on a plate or cake stand. Add half the cream and spread to the edges. Blob the jam over the cream and gently spread a little to the edges (good if it drips down the side!), but be careful not to stir the jam into the cream. Sit the second sponge on top and press down gently.

6. Spoon the cream into the piping bag and pipe concentric circles over the cake, so the top is completely covered (see tip).

7. Using a vegetable peeler, shave peelings of white chocolate on to a plate or sheet of baking paper and scatter over the top. For a special occasion, insert star-shaped cake toppers or cake sparklers into the top of the cake.

Mary's Classic Tips:
* An easy way to break up the chocolate before melting is to give it a few sharp taps on the kitchen worktop before unwrapping it – hey presto, broken chocolate!
* For a smoother, more continuous result, pipe the cream in a spiral, starting from the edge, so that any extra cream will be in the middle.
* A thicker bar of chocolate will give bigger curls as it's easier to shave the chocolate from the edge.

Clementine Cake

SERVES 6–8 / COOK TIME: 1–1¼ hours, plus cooling

1 large or 2 small clementines
  (about 125g/4½oz), peeled
  (see tip)
275g (10oz) cold baking
  spread, plus extra
  for greasing
275g (10oz) caster sugar
275g (10oz) self-raising flour
4 eggs

For the icing
250g (9oz) full-fat
  mascarpone cheese
75g (3oz) butter, softened
175g (6oz) icing sugar, sifted

Prepare Ahead:
Can be assembled up to
8 hours ahead. The icing can
be made up to 3 days ahead,
without the clementine pulp,
and stored in the fridge. Add
the pulp just before finishing
the cake.

Freeze:
The sponges freeze well
(without the icing).

This cake has an impressively well-risen deep sponge, flecked with soft orange peel, and using the whole clementine gives a wonderful moistness. Everyone loves this!

1. You will need two 20cm (8in) round, loose-bottomed sandwich tins. Preheat the oven to 180°C/160°C fan/Gas 4, then grease the tins with baking spread and line each base with a disc of baking paper.

2. Place the clementine(s) in a pan of water and cover with a lid. Bring to the boil, then simmer for 30–40 minutes until soft. Leave to cool, then slice into quarters and remove any pips or bits of pith. Roughly chop and transfer to a bowl.

3. Measure the baking spread, sugar and flour into a bowl and add the eggs. Beat together with an electric hand whisk until light and fluffy, then stir in all but 1 tablespoon of clementine pulp. Divide the mixture into the tins and level the tops.

4. Bake in the oven for about 30–35 minutes until well risen and springy to the touch. Leave to cool in the tins until cold enough to handle, then turn out on to a wire rack to cool down completely. Peel off the lining paper from each sponge (see tip).

5. Meanwhile, make the icing. Whisk the mascarpone, butter and icing sugar together until smooth and fluffy, then stir in the reserved clementine pulp.

6. Place one sponge on a serving plate and spread over half the icing, then sandwich together with the second sponge and spread the remaining icing on top.

Mary's Classic Tips:
* Other orange varieties can be substituted for this recipe, tangerines being the closest alternative.
* To avoid marking the sponges on the wire rack, place them with the paper-lined side down and remove the paper just before sandwiching the cakes together.

Orange Polenta Cake

SERVES 8 / COOK TIME: 1¼ hours

300g (11oz) butter, softened,
  plus extra for greasing
300g (11oz) caster sugar
Juice and finely grated zest
  of 1 orange
4 eggs, beaten
300g (11oz) ground almonds
150g (5oz) dried polenta
  (see tip)
1 tsp baking powder
Icing sugar, for dusting

For the glaze
Juice and finely grated zest
  of 1 small orange
75g (3oz) caster sugar

Prepare Ahead:
Can be made up to a
day ahead.

Freeze:
Freezes well.

This cake batter is quite stiff compared to a normal sponge cake batter. Gluten-free, expect it to be firm and grainy due to its flourless nature and the ground almonds.

1. You will need a 23cm (9in) round, spring-form cake tin. Preheat the oven to 160°C/140°C fan/Gas 3, then grease the tin with butter and line the base with a disc of baking paper.

2. Measure the butter and sugar into a bowl, add the orange zest and beat with an electric hand whisk until pale and fluffy. Whisk in the eggs one at a time, then add the ground almonds, polenta, orange juice and baking powder and carefully fold in until thoroughly combined. Spoon into the prepared tin and level the surface.

3. Bake in the oven for about 1¼ hours or until golden brown and springy to the touch and a skewer inserted into the middle of the cake comes out clean. Allow to cool down a little in the tin for 10 minutes while you make the glaze.

4. Place the orange juice and zest in a small saucepan with the sugar and 2 tablespoons of water. Stir together over a low heat until the sugar has dissolved, then raise the heat and simmer for 4–5 minutes until syrupy. Remove the cake from the tin, then spoon the hot syrup over the warm cake and leave to cool completely (see tip).

5. Serve in wedges dusted with icing sugar and with a dollop of crème fraîche.

Mary's Classic Tips:
* If there is a choice of polenta in the shop, choose a finely ground variety rather than a coarser grain, which would be a bit too rough for this cake.
* Spoon over the warm syrup evenly so that the orange zest decorates the whole surface of the cake.

Seed-Topped Banana Bread

MAKES 2 cakes (each serving 6) / COOK TIME: 30–40 minutes, plus cooling

100g (4oz) baking spread,
  plus extra for greasing
150g (5oz) muscovado sugar
200g (7oz) self-raising flour
1 tsp bicarbonate of soda
2 eggs
2 medium (about 200g/7oz)
  ripe bananas (see tip),
  peeled and mashed

For the topping
25g (1oz) pumpkin seeds
25g (1oz) sunflower seeds
1 tbsp demerara sugar

Prepare Ahead:
Can be made up to a day
ahead and kept in an
airtight container.

Freeze:
The cakes freeze well. Eat
one now and freeze the other
for later.

These lovely well-risen, light-textured moist cakes are perfect for when the bananas are over-ripe in the fruit bowl and no one is keen on eating them! . The seeds and sugar topping adds crunch and nuttiness. Baking two small cakes is perfect when making for school fetes etc. While one goes out the door never to be tasted or seen again, the other can stay at home to please the family!

1. You will need two 450g (1lb) loaf tins (see tip). Preheat the oven to 180°C/160°C fan/Gas 4, then grease the tins with baking spread and line with baking paper.

2. Measure the baking spread, sugar, flour and bicarbonate of soda into a large bowl, add the eggs and bananas and beat with an electric hand whisk until light and combined. Spoon the mixture equally between the prepared tins and level the tops. Sprinkle over the seeds and demerara sugar.

3. Bake both cakes on the middle shelf in the oven for about 35–40 minutes or until well risen, golden and a skewer inserted into the middle of each cake comes out clean.

4. Allow to cool in the tin for 10 minutes and then turn out on to a wire rack and peel off the baking paper before leaving to cool down completely.

Mary's Classic Tips:
* Never throw out even the blackest of bananas. The riper they are, the softer and more flavour they have. Bananas also freeze really well. Once past their best for eating, peel and open freeze on a tray, then pack into freezer bags. You'll always have bananas to hand to make this quick and easy cake – just defrost and use as above.
* To make one large cake, use a 900g (2lb) loaf tin and bake for 50–60 minutes.

Ginger Spiced Ring Cake

SERVES 8 / COOK TIME: 25–35 minutes

175g (6oz) baking spread,
  plus extra for greasing
175g (6oz) self-raising flour
175g (6oz) muscovado sugar
1 tsp baking powder
3 eggs (see tip)
3 tbsp milk
2 tsp ground ginger
1 tsp ground mixed spice
½ tsp ground nutmeg
  (or freshly grated)
1 tsp ground all spice
4 stem ginger bulbs,
  finely chopped

For the icing
100g (4oz) icing sugar, sifted
2–3 tbsp ginger syrup
  (from the jar)
2 stem ginger bulbs,
  finely sliced

Prepare Ahead:
Can be made up to a day
ahead and stored in an
airtight tin. The icing can be
made a few hours in advance;
cover the surface with
greaseproof paper or cling
film to stop a skin forming.

Freeze:
The cake freezes well without
the icing.

This really is impressive, special and such a treat. Perfect for a celebration, I like to serve it over Christmas time. Light, moist and well-risen, it has a lovely combination of spice to complement the stem ginger.

1. You will need a 1.1-litre (2-pint) ring or bundt tin and a piping bag (optional). Preheat the oven 180°C/160°C fan/Gas 4, then grease the tin well with baking spread and line the sides and base of the tin with strips of baking paper (see tip).

2. Place all the cake ingredients in a bowl and beat using an electric hand whisk, or a free-standing food mixer, until smooth and creamy. Spoon into the prepared tin and level the top.

3. Bake in the oven for 25–35 minutes until well risen and just coming away from the sides of the tin. Leave for a few minutes in the tin or until it is cool enough to handle.

4. Carefully loosen the sides of the cake from the tin, and turn on to a wire rack to cool completely, base side down, having removed the baking paper.

5. To make the icing, mix the icing sugar and syrup together until smooth and a drizzling consistency. Add the extra tablespoon of syrup if needed. Place a lined baking tray under the wire rack to catch the drips, then zigzag the icing over the cake with a teaspoon or using a piping bag, and scatter with the ginger slices. Carefully transfer to a plate and cut into slices to serve.

Mary's Classic Tips:
* Room-temperature eggs give the best results for baking.
* Brush the paper strips with melted baking spread, if you like, to help them stick to the tin. Instead of cutting strips of baking paper, another option is to cut out a disc of paper about 5cm (2in) bigger than the tin. Cut out a circle in the middle of the disc and then cut slits in the paper ring to help it fit into the curved base of the tin.

Double Lemon Traybake

MAKES **24 squares** / COOK TIME: 30–35 minutes, plus cooling

225g (8oz) cold baking
   spread, plus extra
   for greasing
225g (8oz) caster sugar
275g (10oz) self-raising flour
2 tsp baking powder (see tip)
4 eggs
2 tbsp milk
2 tbsp lemon curd
Finely grated zest of 2 lemons

For the icing
3–4 tbsp lemon juice
250g (9oz) icing sugar, sifted
Finely grated zest of 1 lemon
   (see tip)

....

Prepare Ahead:
Can be made up to a day
ahead and kept in an
airtight container.

....

Freeze:
The cake freezes well
without the icing.

This is a great cake: it will become your go-to recipe for all the traybakes needed for fetes, coffee mornings, friends moving house etc. The all-in-one method of making, whisked in one bowl, is minimum fuss and super quick. It's easy to ice, transport and will freeze well too, making it a great standby to tuck in the freezer.

1. You will need a 23 x 30cm (9 x 12in) traybake or roasting tin. Preheat the oven to 180°C/160°C fan/Gas 4, then grease the tin with baking spread and line the base with baking paper.

2. Place all the ingredients for the cake into a large bowl and use an electric hand whisk to beat well for about 2 minutes until well blended. Turn the mixture into the prepared tin and level the top.

3. Bake in the oven for about 30–35 minutes or until the cake has shrunk from the sides of the tin and springs back when pressed lightly in the middle with your fingertips. Leave to cool in the tin.

4. Meanwhile, make the icing. In a medium bowl, mix together the lemon juice and icing sugar to give a runny consistency. Use a palette knife to spread out evenly over the cake, sprinkle with the lemon zest and leave to set before cutting into pieces to serve.

Mary's Classic Tips:
* To ensure a lovely level top for the icing, be careful to measure the baking powder accurately – too much and the batter will rise up too quickly and sink on cooling.
* For longer pieces of rind in attractive, curled shapes, use a lemon zester/canelle knife rather than a grater, if you prefer.

Chocolate & Vanilla Swirl Cake

SERVES 8–10 / COOK TIME: 40–45 minutes, plus cooling

225g (8oz) caster sugar
225g (8oz) self-raising flour
225g (8oz) butter, softened,
   plus extra for greasing
1 tsp baking powder
2 tbsp milk
1 tsp vanilla extract
4 eggs
2 tbsp cocoa powder
1–1½ tbsp boiling water
Icing sugar, for dusting

Prepare Ahead:
Can be made up to a
day ahead.

Freeze:
Freezes well.

Mary's Classic Tips:
* Disposable icing bags,
available from most
supermarkets, are the
easiest ones to use here.
Snip a good-sized hole
(2–3cm/¾–1¼in) in the end
of each bag to make nice
wide bands of alternating
colours for the cake.
* Add the boiling water
cautiously, a few drops at a
time, to get to a thick paste
that will mix easily into the
cake batter.

Sometimes called marble cake because of its two colours, this is a plain cake as it has no icing, but is the perfect slice to go with a cuppa. Also good served warmed as a dessert with custard.

1. You will need a 23cm (9in) round, loose-bottomed cake tin and two piping bags, each with a wide plain nozzle or cut end (see tip). Preheat the oven to 180°C/160°C fan/Gas 4, then grease the tin with butter and line the base with a disc of baking paper.

2. Measure the sugar and flour into a large bowl with the butter, baking powder, milk and vanilla extract. Add the eggs and beat with an electric hand whisk until light and smooth.

3. Spoon half of this mixture into a separate bowl. Mix the cocoa paste with enough of the boiling water to make a thick paste (see tip), then stir into the batter in this bowl. Spoon this chocolate mixture into one piping bag and the rest of the cake batter (the vanilla mixture) into the other.

4. Pipe 2 tablespoons of vanilla mixture into the centre of the prepared cake tin to form a circle. Pipe a ring of chocolate mixture around the vanilla. Continue to pipe alternating rings of vanilla and chocolate so it looks like an archery target! If you have any cake mixture left in the piping bags by the time you reach the edge of the tin, go back over some of the rings you have already made.

5. Level the top of the cake and bake in the oven for 40–45 minutes or until well risen and springy to the touch. Leave to cool in the tin for 10 minutes, then remove from the tin and place on a wire rack to cool down completely. Dust with icing sugar to serve.

Rock Cakes

MAKES **12 cakes** / COOK TIME: **12–15 minutes**

225g (8oz) self-raising flour
2 tsp baking powder
1 tsp ground mixed spice
100g (4oz) butter, softened
75g (3oz) demerara sugar,
   plus extra for sprinkling
75g (3oz) sultanas
1 large egg, beaten
3 tbsp milk

Freeze:
These freeze well.

These old-fashioned cakes remind me of my childhood. They should be dry and crumbly and not too sweet. I had forgotten how easy these are to make and what a crowd pleaser they are. Made in the summer hols, they are ideal for picnics and lunchboxes. Kids loved them, adults remember them fondly.

1. Preheat the oven to 200°C/180°C fan/Gas 6 and line a large baking sheet with baking paper.

2. Measure the flour, baking powder, spice and butter into a large bowl. Rub in the butter using your fingertips until the mixture resembles breadcrumbs. Add the sugar and sultanas and mix well.

3. Mix the egg and milk together in a jug, then make a well in the centre of the dry ingredients and pour in the egg mixture. Using a round-ended knife, mix together into a light and airy dough.

4. Either spoon or blob the cake mixture on to the prepared baking sheet to form 12 mounds, spaced well apart, and sprinkle over a little extra sugar.

5. Bake in the oven for 12–15 minutes until risen and lightly golden brown. Cool on a wire rack before serving (see tip).

Mary's Classic Tips:
* Traditional rock cakes are best eaten on the day if possible because they do not keep well as they have a low amount of butter.

Shortbread

MAKES 30 biscuits / COOK TIME: 40 minutes, plus cooling

225g (8oz) plain flour
225g (8oz) butter, plus extra
for greasing
100g (4oz) caster sugar
100g (4oz) semolina
2 tbsp demerara sugar

Prepare Ahead:
Can be made up to 3 days
ahead and kept in
airtight container.

Freeze:
The cooked shortbread
freezes well.

**Shortbread is my ultimate biscuit favourite in every way.
We make it weekly so whenever anyone pops in or we have
work meetings, we have it at hand to share. Delicious, buttery,
simple-but-classic shortbread. The demerara gives it a nice
crunch. Perfect with a cuppa!**

1. You will need a 23 x 33cm (9 x 13in) Swiss roll tin. Preheat
   the oven to 160°C/140°C fan/Gas 3 and lightly grease the tin
   with butter.

2. Measure the flour, butter, caster sugar and semolina into a
   food processor and whizz for a few minutes or just until the
   mixture comes together in a ball of dough.

3. Tip into the prepared tin and, using the back of a spoon,
   push the dough into the tin to make it an even thickness.
   Smooth the surface and sprinkle with demerara sugar.

4. Bake in the oven for 40 minutes or until very pale golden and
   firm to the touch. Leave to cool in the tin for 5 minutes, then
   cut into 30 even-sized pieces (6 x 5 across the tin) and
   transfer to a wire rack to cool down completely (see tip).

Mary's Classic Tip:
* It is important to cut the shortbread while it is still warm and
  then remove the biscuits from the tin as soon as they have
  been cut or they will stick to the tin.

Drop Scones

MAKES 18–24 drop scones / COOK TIME: 2–3 minutes per batch

175g (6oz) self-raising flour
1 tsp baking powder
40g (1½oz) caster sugar
Finely grated zest of
   1 small orange
1 egg
200ml (7fl oz) milk
Sunflower oil, for frying

Serving options
Butter
Maple syrup or honey
Natural Greek yoghurt and
   blueberries or raspberries

Prepare Ahead:
Can be made up to 6 hours
ahead and reheated to serve.
Arrange in a single layer on a
baking tray, cover tightly
with foil and warm through
in a moderate oven for about
10 minutes.

Freeze:
The drop scones freeze well
(see tip); defrost and warm
through as above.

Also known as Scotch Pancakes, these were classically made on a solid metal griddle on an open fire, back in the day. Now it is more practical to use a large non-stick frying pan or if you have an Aga, the simmering plate. Serve as soon as they are made with butter, syrup and jam or fruit and yoghurt.

1. Measure the flour, baking powder and sugar into a large bowl and add the orange zest. Mix together, then make a well in the centre and add the egg and half the milk. Beat well, with a whisk, until you have a smooth, thick batter, then beat in enough of the remaining milk to make a batter the consistency of thick pouring cream.

2. Heat a little oil in a large non-stick frying pan over a high heat. Drop the batter in dessertspoonfuls into the hot pan, spacing each dollop of the mixture well apart to allow it to spread. Cook for about 2 minutes or until bubbles start to appear on the surface, then turn over with a non-stick blunt-ended palette knife or spatula, and cook on the other side for a further 30–60 seconds or until lightly golden brown on both sides.

3. Use the palette knife to lift the scones on to a wire rack, then cover them with a clean tea towel to keep them soft and warm. Continue making more scones in the same way with the remaining batter, adding a splash more oil if the pan gets too dry.

4. Serve at once spread with butter, syrup or honey, or with Greek yoghurt and blueberries or raspberries or other seasonal fruits.

Mary's Classic Tip:
* Before freezing the drop pancakes, wrap them in greaseproof paper and pack in a freezer-proof container to prevent them getting damaged edges.

Feathered Iced Biscuits

MAKES 25 biscuits / COOK TIME: 18–20 minutes, plus cooling and setting

100g (4oz) butter, softened
150g (5oz) caster sugar
1 egg, beaten
250g (9oz) plain flour, plus
  extra for dusting
Finely grated zest of 1 lemon

For the glacé icing
200g (7oz) icing sugar, sifted
3–4 tbsp lemon juice

For the lemon icing
75g (3oz) icing sugar, sifted
1 tbsp lemon juice
Yellow gel natural food
  colouring (see tip)

Very old fashioned and classic, and so very cute!

1. You will need a 7cm (2¾in) fluted pastry cutter and a small disposable piping bag. Preheat the oven to 180°C/160°C fan/Gas 4 (see tip) and line two baking sheets with baking paper.

2. Measure the butter and sugar into a bowl and beat with an electric hand whisk until light and fluffy. Add the egg, then gradually add the flour, followed by the lemon zest, and continue to beat until a dough has formed.

3. Knead gently and then roll out on a floured work surface to the thickness of a £1 coin. Use the pastry cutter to stamp out about 25 pastry discs, then use a palette knife to place on the lined baking sheets, spacing the discs evenly apart.

4. Bake in the oven for 18–20 minutes or until pale golden. Leave for a minute or two on the baking sheet to firm up and then transfer to a wire rack to finish cooling.

5. To make the glacé icing, place the icing sugar in a medium bowl. Add the lemon juice and mix well into a smooth coating consistency.

Continued overleaf →

....

Freeze:
The iced biscuits freeze well.
The unbaked dough can also
be frozen.

6. Place the icing sugar for the lemon icing in a separate bowl. Add the yellow food colouring, a few drops at a time, and mix to an even colour (see tip).

7. When the biscuits are cool, cover the tops with the glacé icing. Spoon the yellow icing into the piping bag and snip a very small amount off the end. Pipe yellow stripes across the biscuits and then lightly drag the point of a cocktail stick across the icing lines to give a feathered effect. Leave the iced biscuits to set firm (see tip).

Mary's Classic Tips:
* You will need two shelves at the top of the oven to bake these biscuits evenly, so make sure they are positioned correctly before you start cooking.
* Add plenty of yellow food colouring to the lemon icing – it needs to be a nice bright shade to stand out against the white icing once it has been feathered.
* Once the biscuits are iced, the glacé icing will take several hours to dry completely and become 'knock-proof'. Be patient before piling them into a storage tin; once dried they are quite hardy, but stack them too soon and the pretty icing will be spoiled.

Honey Melts

MAKES about 25 biscuits / CHILLING TIME: 1 hour / COOK TIME: 10 minutes per batch

100g (4oz) icing sugar
125g (4½oz) butter, softened
3 egg whites
1 tbsp runny honey
125g (4½oz) plain flour,
   plus extra for dusting

Freeze:
These freeze well; refresh in
the oven to serve.

A delicate biscuit similar to langues du chat French biscuits, but easier to make. These biscuits are really little, thin sponge cakes – like the base of jaffa cakes – rather than crisp biscuits.

1. Measure the icing sugar and butter into a large bowl and beat with an electric hand whisk until light and fluffy (see tip). Add the egg whites, one by one, beating well between each addition. Don't worry if the mixture looks a little curdled with each addition – keep beating to bring it back together.

2. Stir in the honey, then fold in the flour to make a smooth paste. Cover with cling film and chill in the fridge for about an hour.

3. Meanwhile, preheat the oven 180°C/160°C fan/Gas 4 and line four baking sheets with baking paper. Alternatively, line two baking sheets and cook the biscuits in two batches.

4. On a work surface lightly dusted with flour, roll the mixture into about 25 balls each the size of a walnut (see tip). Arrange on the baking sheets, spacing them apart to allow them to spread during cooking.

5. Bake in the oven for about 10 minutes until golden brown and tinged slightly darker around the edges. Once cooked, leave to firm up on the baking sheets for a couple of minutes, before transferring to a wire rack to cool.

Mary's Classic Tips:
* When beating the icing sugar and butter together, start the whisk on a slow setting, to prevent clouds of powdery icing sugar escaping from the bowl. Once all the sugar has been incorporated into the butter, you can increase to a high speed.
* Use a rounded teaspoon measure or melon baller to help you shape the mixture into balls.

COOK'S
NOTES

Mary's Classic Recipe Finder

In this book you'll find a recipe to suit every occasion – from classic family suppers and recipes that can be made ahead and frozen to more extravagant meals for entertaining. We've designed this recipe finder to help you find exactly what you're looking for.

Family favourites

Timeless recipes, which will please all the family, young and old!

Quick and easy puddings and treats

When your sweet tooth calls, these are quick to whip up, and always satisfying.

Fresh from the garden

For those lucky enough to have a garden, these recipes are perfect for enjoying your produce.

Cook's Notes

Weighing and Measuring

* When you're using the recipes in this book, you're welcome to make little tweaks of your own. While it's best to follow exact weights where these are given first time round, next time you make the recipes, you could use a bit more or a bit less to suit your taste. Equally, you might prefer to substitute one type of cheese for another in a recipe or use a different kind of fish or meat. Feel free to experiment.

* Both metric and imperial measures are provided. When you're weighing out ingredients, it's best to go by one or the other – never mix the two. (See also the Conversion Tables on pages 308–309.)

* Spoon measures are level unless otherwise stated.

* In recipes for cakes and other baked items, the ingredients need to be measured carefully. I find that digital scales are best for the purpose.

* For oven temperatures, the standard Centigrade measure is given first, followed by the fan temperature, 20 degrees less in each case. (See also the Conversion Tables on pages 308–309.) As ovens vary in the amount of heat they produce, you may need to cook a dish for slightly more or less time, depending on your own particular oven. It can be helpful to use an oven thermometer to gauge the correct temperature for cooking a dish.

* Where a type of cooking oil isn't specified, you can use any oil that you like, although it's best to choose something relatively mild, such as sunflower oil, that won't overpower the flavour of the dish. For dressings, use the best-quality oil that you can afford, to give the most intense flavour.

* Try to buy the best-quality meat and fish that you can afford – free range, in the case of meat, and sustainably sourced fish. Check with your fishmonger, or at the fish counter in your local supermarket, and use an alternative type of fish if you find that the kind you have selected is no longer on the sustainability list – which changes according to fish stock levels.

* Eggs are large, unless otherwise stated, and I prefer free range, if possible.

* I use granulated sugar for general sweetening; caster sugar, which is finer, for baking; and icing sugar for icing. Light muscovado gives a great flavour and demerara creates delicious crunchy toppings and adds a fudgy flavour to cakes and puddings. All these sugars keep for long periods in sealed containers. If you find after a time the sugar has become a solid block in the bag, store a clean, damp J-cloth in the bag to separate the grains.

* Modern milling techniques mean that it is not always necessary to sift flour – I always specify in a recipe where it is needed.

* To turn plain flour into self-raising flour, add 2–3 teaspoons of baking powder to every 200g (7oz) of plain flour. Check the sell-by dates on flour and baking powder.

Quantities

Over the years, I have been fortunate enough to have given many large parties at home and in the garden, and I have learnt that the more people you have, the less they seem to eat! Most people cook far more than they need to, and I always feel that it is a shame to be so wasteful. Below is a rough quantities calculator that I use to work out recipes for my events. Of course, quantities will vary slightly depending on your guests, the time of day and the type of party you are hosting.

Savoury dishes, per person:
Joint with bone: 175–225g (6–8oz)
Joint without bone: 100–175g (4–6oz)
Meat for casseroles: 175g (6oz)
Pasta, uncooked: 75–100g (3–4oz)
Rice, uncooked: 40–50g (1½–2oz)
Salmon: 100–125g (4–4½oz)
Smoked salmon: 75g (3oz)
Soup: 600ml (1 pint) will serve 3 people
Fillet steak: 150g (5oz)
Other steaks: 175–200g (6–7 oz)

Sweet dishes, per person:
Cakes: a 20cm (8in) sponge will feed 6–8
Meringues: 1 egg white and 50g (2oz) caster sugar will make
    about 5 small meringues
Soft fruits: 75–100g (3–4oz)
Cream to accompany desserts: 600ml (1 pint) per 12 portions

Nibbles, per person:
Crisps: 25g (1oz)
Salted nuts: 15g (½oz)

Sandwiches and bread:
1 loaf, medium cut, makes 10 rounds of sandwiches
100g (4oz) butter is enough for 1 large sandwich loaf or 12
    bread rolls
1 long baguette cuts into 20 slices

Drinks:
Champagne: 1 bottle (75cl) will serve 6 full glasses (8 if pouring
    smaller measures)
Wine: 1 bottle (75cl) will serve 6 glasses
Soft drinks and mixers: 1 bottle (1 litre) will serve 6 glasses
Milk for coffee: allow 900ml (1½ pints) per 20 cups
Milk for tea: allow 600ml (1 pint) per 20 cups

Advice on Freezing

The freezer is an essential in a modern kitchen, and it would certainly have been difficult for me to cope with feeding a family or entertaining if I could not have prepared a number of recipes in advance, freezing them until needed. I also hate waste, so instead of leaving them in the fridge hoping they will be used up quickly, I try to freeze leftovers. The trick to using your freezer wisely is to keep a note of everything you have in there. I keep mine as a list stuck on the inside of my kitchen cupboard. Look at your list before you make a meal and cross items off when they have been eaten.

What you can freeze

Main courses
I find it invaluable to freeze meals for supper or dinner parties, and will often double up a recipe to make one dish to eat now and one for another time. Most cooked dishes are best frozen for no longer than 3 months so they retain their original flavour.

Vegetables
They do taste better fresh, but vegetables can be a useful thing to have in the freezer. Most vegetables need to be blanched before freezing as this helps to retain their colour, texture, flavour and the vitamins within them. Plunge them into boiling water and cook for 1–3 minutes, then immediately drain and plunge into ice-cold water. Certain watery vegetables, such as cucumber, endives, lettuce, radishes and artichokes, cannot be frozen. Tomatoes can be frozen but are only suitable to add to casseroles as they become very watery.

Fruit
Most freeze well and make an excellent stand-by dessert. Apples, rhubarb, plums, peaches, cherries and gooseberries are best stewed with a little sugar. Soft fruits such as strawberries or peaches are best turned into purées as the whole frozen fruit will turn mushy when you defrost them. Smaller fruits like raspberries, blackberries, blackcurrants and redcurrants can be frozen whole.

Cakes and puddings
Anything with delicate icing or decoration (such as piped cupcakes) should be open frozen so that it is not damaged when wrapped or packaged. To open freeze, spread the items out on a tray and place in the freezer. When they are completely frozen, they can be packed in containers or bags without damaging the shape.

Biscuit and pastry dough
Biscuit dough can be frozen in a log shape, ready to be defrosted in the fridge then sliced and baked. Pastry cases can be frozen unbaked or baked blind ready to fill. Uncooked pastry freezes perfectly for up to 3 months.

Milk, cream and butter
It is useful to keep milk in the freezer; as if you run out, it can be easily defrosted in a sink of cold water. The milk and fat will separate, but will homogenise again when shaken. Single cream and yoghurt do not freeze, but double and clotted cream do freeze as they have a higher fat content. Freeze cream for up to 3 months only. Butter and hard cheese (ideally grated so it is ready to use) are also useful to keep in the freezer – again for only 3 months. Leftover cheese with a high fat content will freeze well, such as brie or stilton. Buttercream icing does freeze well, but use after 3 months or the flavour will deteriorate.

Eggs
Whole eggs do not freeze well, so do not add them to a fish pie if you are freezing it. Egg whites can be frozen in small containers (make sure you label how many you have frozen) and are ideal for meringues. Egg yolks can also be frozen in small containers to enrich sauces or omelettes at a later date.

Wine
Wine can be frozen in ice cube trays ready to add to sauces. When frozen, decant into small bags to store.

Jars of sauces
If you have half a jar of any pasta sauce, roasted red peppers or pesto left over, decant into containers and freeze. Passata and chopped tomatoes also freeze well if you have some spare.

Do not freeze

Raw meat and fish that has already been frozen
To prevent the quality from deteriorating, it is always best
not to refreeze anything that has been frozen previously.
However, if it is in perfect condition, it should be safe when
defrosted thoroughly.

Pavlova and meringue
Cooked meringues or pavlova will keep well in an airtight
container, so there is no need to freeze them. Store in a cool
place for up to two months.

Salad ingredients
Ingredients like cucumber and lettuce contain too much water
to freeze well, and would turn mushy once defrosted.

Fresh basil, coriander and dill
It is better to make herbs into pesto or herb butters and freeze
those instead.

Potatoes
If you are making a cottage pie or fish pie with mashed potato,
add less milk and more butter to the potato or it will become
watery when defrosted.

General freezer guidance

* For food safety reasons, cool foods completely after cooking or blanching before freezing.

* Exclude as much air as possible from packaged foods to prevent them drying out, and use the correct-sized container if possible.

* Keep washed cartons from ready-made foods. I wash out and keep ice cream and soup cartons that have tight-fitting lids as these are so useful for freezing portions of food.

* Double wrap foods in foil first, then in a freezer bag. This will help prevent them from being damaged while frozen.

* Always date and label the packages, and add cooking/ reheating instructions too.

* Organise the shelves. Try to keep the same sorts of foods together in sections of your freezer. For example, keep vegetables in one drawer, desserts and cakes in another and so on. Try to keep a good rotation of stock, using up the oldest foods first. Keep all the small ingredients that will easily get lost in one area of the fridge (e.g. chillies, fresh herbs, cubes of stock or wine).

Defrosting

* For best results, always defrost foods in the fridge, otherwise use the defrost setting on the microwave.

* You can defrost casseroles or soups on the hob, but stir thoroughly during defrosting to ensure they're heated through evenly.

* Meat, fish and poultry must reach boiling point for 10 minutes in the centre (3–4 minutes in the microwave) to ensure they are cooked thoroughly.

* Most vegetables can be cooked from frozen.

* Some meals can be cooked from frozen: follow any specific guidance in the recipe, but generally increase the cooking time in the recipe by half again and ensure the centre of the food has reached boiling point for at least 10 minutes before serving.

* If defrosting in the microwave, ensure food is of even thickness or it will cook unevenly.

Conversions & Measurements

Measurements

METRIC	IMPERIAL
5mm	¼in
1cm	½in
2.5cm	1in
5cm	2in
7.5cm	3in
10cm	4in
12.5cm	5in
15cm	6in
18cm	7in
20cm	8in
23cm	9in
25cm	10in
30cm	12in

Oven temperatures

°C	FAN°C	°F	GAS MARK
140°C	Fan 120°C	275°F	Gas 1
150°C	Fan 130°C	300°F	Gas 2
160°C	Fan 140°C	325°F	Gas 3
180°C	Fan 160°C	350°F	Gas 4
190°C	Fan 170°C	375°F	Gas 5
200°C	Fan 180°C	400°F	Gas 6
220°C	Fan 200°C	425°F	Gas 7
230°C	Fan 210°C	450°F	Gas 8
240°C	Fan 220°C	475°F	Gas 9

Volume		Weights	
METRIC	IMPERIAL	METRIC	IMPERIAL
25ml	1fl oz	15g	½oz
50ml	2fl oz	25g	1oz
85ml	3fl oz	40g	1½oz
100ml	3½fl oz	50g	2oz
150ml	5fl oz (¼ pint)	75g	3oz
200ml	7fl oz	100g	4oz
300ml	10fl oz (½ pint)	150g	5oz
450ml	15fl oz (¾ pint)	175g	6oz
600ml	1 pint	200g	7oz
700ml	1¼ pints	225g	8oz
900ml	1½ pints	250g	9oz
1 litre	1¾ pints	275g	10oz
1.2 litres	2 pints	350g	12oz
1.25 litres	2¼ pints	375g	13oz
1.5 litres	2½ pints	400g	14oz
1.6 litres	2¾ pints	425g	15oz
1.75 litres	3 pints	450g	1lb
1.8 litres	3¼ pints	550g	1¼lb
2 litres	3½ pints	675g	1½lb
2.1 litres	3¾ pints	750g	1¾lb
2.25 litres	4 pints	900g	2lb
2.75 litres	5 pints	1.5kg	3lb
3.4 litres	6 pints	1.75kg	4lb
3.9 litres	7 pints	2.25kg	5lb
4.5 litres	8 pints (1 gallon)		

Index

Thank you

Lucy Young, by my side for 28 years, masterminding this book from start to finish. I cannot do what I do without her. We are a team and steer through our busy working lives together with fun and laughter. Luc is always there telling me to slow down, but she says it with a twinkle in her eye, as she knows I love everyday I spend with our little team, striving to make the recipes the best ever.

Lucinda McCord, 17 years testing recipes with Luc and I, with great precision, knowledge and utter loveliness, a treasure to us all.

To Lizzy Gray, from BBC Books, thank you for commissioning the book, and Charlotte Macdonald for editing and co-ordinating it, so easy to work with and a book we are so proud of.

To the A team – Georgia Glynn Smith, for the stunning photography and front cover. One of our most favourites and her creative eye is always looking for the new thing. To Lisa Harrison and Isla Murray, home economists for the shoot and TV – second to none, they are simply the best. We are lucky to have them.

Thanks to Louise Evans for the stunning book design, and Two Associates for the cover artwork, Polly Webb-Wilson for the beautiful props, and Jan Stevens and Anne Harnan for the extra recipe testing.

To our agents, literary agent Felicity Bryan and Joanna Kaye at KBJ – we have the perfect support, thank you so much.

Karen Ross from Sidney St who produced the accompanying TV series – Emma Boswell, Dave Crearer and our great team, working year after year to create the very best programme for the viewers.

I am always so amazed and flattered by the support our readers and viewers give us. Thank you, thank you, I love what I do because of you.

Mary Berry

1 3 5 7 9 10 8 6 4 2

BBC Books, an imprint of Ebury Publishing
20 Vauxhall Bridge Road,
London SW1V 2SA

BBC Books is part of the Penguin Random House group of companies
whose addresses can be found at global.penguinrandomhouse.com

Photography by Georgia Glynn Smith

This book is published to accompany the television series entitled
Classic Mary Berry first broadcast on BBC Two in 2018.
Classic Mary Berry is a Sidney Street TV production.

BBC Commissioning Executive: David Brindley
Series Director: David Crerar
Series Producers: Antonia Lloyd and Emma Boswell
Executive producer: Karen Ross
Production Managers: Kaz Cranston and Bethany Medcalf
Production Co-ordinator: Mary Mullarkey

First published by BBC Books in 2018

www.eburypublishing.co.uk

A CIP catalogue record for this book is available from the British Library

ISBN 9781785943249

Publishing Director: Lizzy Gray
Project Editor: Charlotte Macdonald
Food Stylist: Lisa Harrison
Prop Stylist: Polly Webb Wilson
Design: Louise Evans
Testing: Jan Fullwood, Anne Harnan
Copyeditor: Kate Parker

Colour origination by Altaimage, London
Printed and bound in Germany by Mohn Media GmbH

Penguin Random House is committed to a sustainable future for our
business, our readers and our planet. This book is made from Forest
Stewardship Council® certified paper.